Affluent Marketing Blueprint

Affluent Marketing Blueprint

Secrets of Confidently Selling to Millionaires & Billionaires

by Mark Satterfield

To get the companion video series for free, simply visit
www.AffluentMarketingBlueprint.com
or scan this QR code:

Mandalay Press

ISBN: 979-8-9876017-0-9

To my wife, Marian, for all her love,
support and encouragement.

TABLE OF CONTENTS

Introduction

Bank robber Willie Sutton allegedly said that he robbed banks because "That's where the money is." The same principle applies in business. There's not a whole lot of benefit in selling to poor people, but there's a lot to be had in selling to the rich, and that's what this book is about: how to sell practically anything to people who are very wealthy.

It doesn't matter if you yourself are wealthy or not. That's not a requirement. What is required is that you develop a deep understanding of the mindset of the rich and that you learn what they like, what they loath, what they desire, and what they fear. Equipped with this knowledge and some creative marketing strategies, you can build long-term, extremely profitable relationships with the very affluent. I can say this with confidence because my team and I have worked for the past thirty years with businesses in over two dozen niche industries, and we've successfully marketed their products and services to extremely wealthy clients.

I'll assume that if you're reading this, you have a desire to attract more affluent clients. You may have an established business that already caters to the wealthy and is seeking to expand. Alternatively, you may not yet have any wealthy clients but realize that these are the types of people you want to attract.

Rather than give you a cookie-cutter approach, my goal is to provide you with a variety of options. Everyone is different, and one person may feel comfortable doing what another may not. In the pages that follow, I'll share how to mentally prepare yourself for selling to the affluent as well as practical strategies to getting them to engage with you.

Look, I get it. Building relationships with the very rich can be intimidating, especially if you yourself are not wealthy or if you are just starting out in your career. However, once you have a plan in place for how to attack this segment of the market, you will become more confident, and once you have a few success stories under your belt, the momentum will build upon itself.

The wealthy are a tribe, and like most tribes, they are very skeptical of outsiders. Not surprisingly, they want very little to do with the masses. Once you understand the culture of affluence, you'll become both more comfortable and more effective in cultivating these relationships.

Next, we'll move on to creating your plan for success. My goal here is again to equip you with a variety of options, and I think the best way to do that is by sharing success stories from a diverse group of businesses. You'll meet Larry G., who has built an extremely successful luxury travel agency on the back of "being the guy to know if you want to get connected to virtually anyone."

You'll also meet one of my favorite success stories who was once too scared to strike up a conversation with wealthy patrons, but who now attributes most of his new clients to networking events.

Branding plays a key role in successfully attracting new business. However, branding means something unique in the world of affluent marketing. We'll take a look at what goes into creating a brand that resonates with the super-rich.

You may think that direct mail can't possibly work with this group, but you'd be wrong. Never underestimate the power of a targeted, professional letter. There's a three-letter sequence that has been proven effective time and time again. You'll be able to readily adapt the templates I share with you to virtually any business.

What about advertising? Can you get a viable return on your investment? Yes you can, but not by using traditional image-focused advertising which, ironically, makes up the vast majority of ads one sees in luxury magazines. However, if you use a technique borrowed from the great marketing copywriters, you'll generate substantial returns from your ads both online and off.

Networking is a key element for building relationships with the affluent. You'll hear from Frank Guiffre, who has taught his team how to be extraordinarily successful by employing one special technique. It's absolutely genius, and you'll wonder why you didn't think about applying it years ago. If you've ever felt uncomfortable in a networking or social situation, it will be one of your key takeaways from this book.

I don't want to spoil the fun by going into too much detail this early in our journey together, but suffice it to say you'll find a wealth of strategies and tactics (along with some well deserved motivation) that will enable you to successfully achieve the goals I know you have. I do have one caveat: as you read this book, I encourage you to keep an open mind. I'll be discussing affluent marketing strategies in a variety of industries. If you're a financial advisor, don't immediately skip over the examples from fields such as concierge medicine or private jet leasing. What I've learned over the years is that what works well in one industry can usually be adapted and successfully implemented in many others.

And please, don't say to yourself, "This won't work, none of my competitors are doing it." The last thing you want to do is mimic what your competition does. It is very hard to get the attention of the wealthy, so you'll need to think creatively.

So, with all that in mind, let's begin.

Chapter 1:
Who they are

1.1 Meet the affluent

People can be classified into two groups: the rich and the not-rich. If you're rich, then you're part of the tribe. You may have grown up wealthy, or through hard work and, let's admit it, a certain amount of luck, you're now a part of the top one to three percent. If you're not rich, that means that the wealthy are a bit of an unknown to you. You likely have some preconceived notions about them, some of which are probably right, but a lot which are significantly wrong. Regardless of which group you're in, I think you'll find what follows to be helpful.

Is marketing to the wealthy for you? The odds are good that it is. First of all, the affluent market is larger than you might think. Although the affluent may appear to be a very small demographic, this is actually somewhat deceiving. We can measure the affluent by either household income or net worth. According to Marke-tResearch.com, a commonly accepted breakdown is as follows:

> Mass affluent adults are defined as adults in households with an income of $100,000-$149,999. Highly affluent adults are those with a household income of $150,000-$249,999. Super-affluent consumers are adults in households with a household income of $250,000 or more.
>
> The 34 million mass affluent consumers represent 15% of all American consumers, while the highly affluent account for 9% and the super-affluent segment amounts to 4% of American adults.

Clearly, the affluent niche is larger than most people think, and it's growing. Despite the size of this niche, however, there are still a number of myths about the wealthy, and it's important that we understand these myths if we are going to be successful.

Do I have to be rich to successfully sell to the wealthy? The short answer is no, you don't. You have to understand their customs and mindset, but you don't have to be at the same level of income as your prospective clients in order to do business with them.

Aren't rich people snobby? Sort of. Wealthy people, especially those that are self-made, see themselves as superior in the sense that they have bucked the odds and achieved outsized business success. The vast majority of rich people made their money by starting and growing a business. It may not have been particularly glamorous. My next door neighbor made a fortune in paper clips.

When thinking about entrepreneurs, however, it's important to keep in mind that most businesses never see their fifth anniversary. Of the businesses that survive, very few achieve the type of success necessary to make the founder a millionaire. Successful founders take an enormous and largely justified pleasure in what they've achieved against huge odds. To those who have not had that experience, such attitudes can at times come across as snobby.

Successful entrepreneurs tend not to have an enormous amount of patience, and they usually don't tolerate fools. Again, this can sometimes appear brusque to outsiders. What they most often want are products and services that will make their lives easier. Since the affluent are a tribe, they are also desirous of goods and services that others in their world have. It's sort of like the notion of "keeping up with the Jones" on steroids.

This is why it is very difficult to market to both the "masses and the upper classes" as my great-aunt Caroline would say. Barriers have broken down somewhat over the years, but there are still *certain* brands, *certain* neighborhoods, *certain* designers, *certain* advisors, *certain* fill-in-the-blanks that the affluent gravitate toward. Our role is thus to become one of the "*certains.*"

It's important to keep in mind that this tribal herding around certain providers is driven by insecurity as much as anything else. The rich, especially those that are suddenly wealthy due to a liquidity event of some sort, have a strong desire to be accepted by their new peer group. They want to make the safe choice. It's our job as marketers to position our products and services in a way that resonates with that desire.

They worry about things such as their children's education and wellbeing, their own inevitable aging, and being left behind.

Also, although you might not guess it, they are often concerned about being perceived as fakes, or about not being recognized for their success.

Flipping this around, one of the most positive traits about the rich is that they are most often intensely curious, particularly about people. Many younger professionals worry that they won't have anything interesting to say to someone who is significantly older or wealthier than they are. They worry that they have nothing in common, and that may be true, but it misses the point.

If they find you interesting, they will take you into their group. One of the keys to being interesting is being a good conversationalist, and the secret to being a good conversationalist is simply to ask good questions. I'm going to equip you with some great questions to ask as we move forward on this journey together.

More than anything else, the rich love being rich. While they share many similarities with all of us, there are distinctions that make them unique. Let's learn more about those next.

1.2 The rich are different from those who aren't

In 1926, F. Scott Fitzgerald wrote that the rich "are different from you and me," to which Ernest Hemingway supposedly replied, "Yes, they have more money." While that's certainly true, the wealthy and super affluent also have unique traits that set them apart. Understanding what these are enables you to position your products or services in a way that separates you from others in your field.

It's important to remember that the rich are a tight-knit

tribe. Assuming you've already built a relationship, doing business with the affluent depends on how well you communicate your offer in a way that appeals to them directly. Remember, the more the affluent see a reflection of themselves in your marketing, the greater the chance they'll stop and check it out. Let's take a look at some of the common traits rich people share and discuss ways you can position yourself for maximum acceptance.

First, the super-rich are nonconformists, and wealthy people enjoy swimming against the tide. One of key findings in *The Wealth Elite*, Rainer Zitelmann's famous doctoral study of the wealthy, was that the affluent enjoy being contrarian. Breaking through the noise of everyday life is a huge problem when marketing any product or service. Leveraging a contrarian approach in your marketing is a very effective way to get attention, and seeking to appeal to the contrarian nature of the wealthy can lead to some interesting ideas for marketing your products or services.

Mark Twain famously said, "It's not what you don't know that gets you in trouble—it's what you know that just ain't so," and Kevin Trudeau was one of the first to capitalize on this concept with books like *The Weight Loss Cure "They" Don't Want You To Know About*. Although Trudeau's claims were largely unsubstantiated and he was later charged with fraud, the claim that what you believe is wrong was highly effective marketing.

Using the phrase "What you believe is wrong" or a variation of it is particularly effective with the wealthy. They have no problem contradicting prevailing opinions and often build their fortunes by going against the grain. More importantly, stating what they believe may be wrong is a great attention getter.

Let's apply this concept to your product or service. What common belief can you identify that either is wrong or perhaps creates more problems than it solves? Once you've identified a few of these, you can use the following types of headlines in your marketing:

- Lies you've been told about (a topic of interest)
- What (so-and-so expert) doesn't want you to know about (a topic of interest)
- Why (a common solution) causes (problems rather than solutions)

A financial advisor in Dallas used this approach very effectively with a direct mail campaign she sent to millennial millionaires. Above the letter's salutation was the headline "Why the Traditional Baby Boomer 60/40 Stock to Bond Allocation Is Actually Costing You Money. Key Findings From Our Most Recent Study Reveal the Ideal Portfolio for Millennials." The rate of response to this mailing was double what she had achieved in the past. She told me:

> I think its success was the result of three things. First was the fear many millennials have of being lumped in with the older baby boomer generation. Second, there was a high curiosity factor about my debunking what is traditionally seen as a very safe

> and traditional asset model allocation. Finally, the fact that we had done a study of people just like them made them highly curious about the solution we recommended. Quite frankly, I was pleasantly surprised at the response, and I attribute it to going against the prevailing beliefs.

Let's move on to the next trait of wealthy people: the rich believe that the realization of personal potential is the key to happiness. This is particularly true for the self-made entrepreneurs. Many of the very wealthy that we work with will admit that at some point there comes an "Is this all there is?" moment. This often results in them embarking on a quest to fill in the gaps they may have in their knowledge or education.

One of our clients started selling cars at the age of eighteen. With little more than a high school education, he eventually built a car empire that included nine extremely successful dealerships. He told me:

> When I was starting out, I definitely had a bit of a chip on my shoulder. My attitude was that I was just as good as those people who had fancy MBAs. I wore my lack of formal education as some sort of badge of honor. However, an interesting thing happened after I started to make a lot of money.
>
> Since I was rich, I'd get invited to these charity events where I'd rub shoulders with other extremely

> wealthy people. What I noticed was that they were able to talk about a wide range of subjects that I had no knowledge about. Now, don't get me wrong. I'm extremely proud of what I've achieved, especially given where I started from, but I started to want more.
>
> And by more, I'm not talking about stuff. I bought the houses, the boat, and all the other things that you buy when you start making serious money. What I found really interesting was that there were a lot of guys like me. They didn't have a lot of formal education, but they had all these outside interests that they were really knowledgeable and passionate about. I wanted that.

How can you use this to your advantage? In every face-to-face sales situation, there comes the time when you get to talk about your background. Instead of solely focusing on your track record or your success and your knowledge, you also want to communicate the obstacles you've overcome to get to where you are today. You will find that the wealthy are particularly impressed by these stories. For example, one of our clients who struggled to build a relationship with a high tech entrepreneur finally broke through when she told him about her early struggles and how she became emancipated from her parents at the age of sixteen.

In a similar vein, you want to include your "origin story" on your website. This is a missed opportunity for many businesses. While you don't want to go overboard and make your background sound like something out of Dickens, adding color and context to your bio is extremely effective for catching the attention of the affluent market.

What else sets the affluent apart? The ultra affluent put a greater emphasis on the education of their children than those from the middle class do. Rich parents will research the ratings of schools and where matriculating students go after graduation. Often, they are not impressed. This makes private schools the only viable option, and this has made the competitiveness over admission to these schools skyrocket in recent years. For example, with the recent relocation of a number of financial services firms to South Florida, the number of applications to some K-12 schools is up 109% compared to just a year ago.

How does knowing this benefit you? There are many ways to make yourself invaluable to affluent people. Think about what other services you could offer that would benefit the children of the rich. A number of years ago, we worked with a client in the financial services field who decided to establish an etiquette and career management symposium at a very prestigious private school in Europe. Wealthy parents who were worried about their children acclimating into society were eager to sign their students up.

Dorothy Lang, the wife of a hedge fund CEO, described what motivated her extreme interest in the symposium by saying:

> I think I was probably the first mother to enroll our kids in the program. Both Steven and I come from modest backgrounds, so we are fundamentally

> rooted in solid, Midwestern values. The same isn't exactly true for our kids. Now don't get me wrong, I love them to death, but they've had this life of luxury handed to them on the proverbial silver platter. I really worry about how they are going to interact with kids from different social and economic backgrounds once they get out of the cocoon of private schools. I see these other kids who, quite frankly, act like brats, and it scares Steven and I. The symposium was a great first step in the right direction.

Did this pay off for the sponsor of the program? Let's hear from Toby Galloway, who owns five high-end art galleries in London:

> The culmination of the program was a social event held in the ballroom of a local hotel. It gave the students an opportunity to demonstrate some of their newly acquired social skills, and each of them was required to speak about the specific benefit they got from the symposium. What was interesting and a bit surprising to me was that every parent of the kids showed up for the event. This reinforced my belief that wealthy parents are concerned about how their kids will acclimate into the world at large.
>
> For me personally, it gave me the opportunity as the primary sponsor to make an introductory ad-

> dress. Although it was clear who I worked for and the nature of the work I do, there was absolutely no soliciting of business at the event. That would have been extremely counterproductive. However, since the event went extremely well, and I was now a "known" person, it left the door open to follow up.
>
> What we did that I think was smart was that we took the long-game approach in our follow up. We didn't rush into requesting a meeting to discuss the services of our firm. Instead, the follow up focused on the program and the long-term benefits the kids got from it. We wanted to make sure that we communicated a message that we were committed to the symposium and wanted to do everything we could to make it successful.
>
> Those conversations greased the wheels (to put it inelegantly), and eventually, when I felt the time was right, I was able to seamlessly shift the conversation to how our firm might be successful. Without divulging specific numbers and looking at it as a two-years' investment of time, money and effort, what I can tell you is that the program was extremely successful.

Another client of ours in the private banking sector worked to develop relationships with headmasters of private schools to help facilitate the admissions process for children of his affluent clients. Other financial advisors compiled a list of tutors and coaches who could help the children of wealthy parents improve academically and socially. Insurance broker Malcomb Ribovitz said:

> Look, no one can guarantee that their kid will get into a particular school, but what we can do is help facilitate the process of figuring out what's important to these schools. We put together a half-day seminar at the Harvard Club and invited a select group of parents to attend. I figured we'd get the moms, but a lot of the dads also showed up, which was surprising since these are really busy people.
>
> The program went really well. One school emphasized the importance of team sports while another talked at great lengths about their focus on the arts. A third one talked about the spokes of a wheel and their mission to graduate well rounded students. That's very useful information to have, particularly when writing one's essay or during the interview.
>
> Most importantly, and from a purely business development perspective, the parents thought the program was really valuable. Best of all, when I followed up with the parents, I was now someone they knew. There was a lot of goodwill I accrued that eventually translated into business.

That leads me to a main theme of this chapter: instinct. The super-rich are more likely than others to make decisions based on gut feelings. This means that first impressions carry more weight with the wealthy. While we all have the tendency to judge the proverbial book by its cover, first impressions carry even greater weight with the wealthy. How you look, speak, and carry yourself is of utmost importance. I'll discuss this in more detail shortly.

1.3 The affluent are a tribe

Of all the niche markets out there, the affluent niche is probably the most tribal. The affluent want to associate with each other. They also want to do business with the same people that their peers do business with, or at least with people who are somewhat familiar to them.

The notion of "somewhat familiar" is key. They may not have met you before, or perhaps they know you casually or have seen you at the places they frequent. Maybe they've heard about you in passing, have read an article you wrote, or have seen you interviewed. Somehow, you're on their radar.

You're not necessarily a member of their core group, but you may know some of the same people. They might say, "Yes, I think I've heard of him (or her)," although they can't quite put their finger on precisely where they heard of you. In other words, you're on the periphery of the tribe. You're connected by gossamer strands, but interestingly, that's enough.

Hear me now and believe me later: before you market to the affluent (and market to them you must), you need to be connected, even if ever so slightly, to the tribe. The rich don't trust new people, and because they're rich, that skepticism is warranted. You need to be someone that they've heard of or met or your marketing messages will simply bounce off of them like raindrops on cement.

My grandmother, who (bless her heart) traced her ancestry to the Mayflower, would commonly ask, "Do we know him?" This was her way of ascertaining whether the person was a member of the tribe. Grandmother was a terrible snob, but she wasn't alone. I think the rich today tend to hide their tribalism a bit better, and the language may have changed, but the screening is still the same. When you meet a high-net-worth individual in a casual context, you'll notice that the questions you're asked are meant to determine whether you are a member of the tribe.

Keep in mind, though, that for the purposes of doing business with the very wealthy, being a member of the tribe does not mean you have to be rich yourself. If you want to marry their sons or daughters, then the rules might be different, and you probably do actually have to be wealthy to gain approval. However, that's not what we're focused on here, and the bar is a bit lower for doing business.

Becoming familiar to the affluent, or at least known by a member of the tribe, requires the long game, which is why so few are successful. Don't place too much emphasis on selling services now. Instead, lay the groundwork to later tap into the mother lode of affluent referrals. That's the beauty of this: since the rich are so tribal and so skeptical of those they don't know, they refer like crazy. This is why you first and foremost need to become connected with the tribe.

1.4 Identifying your ideal client

Obviously, the wealthy are bombarded with marketing and sales pitches. It quickly becomes a roar of white noise that none of them pay attention to. The question is, therefore, how can we get the rich to pay attention to *you*?

One way is to make sure your marketing and sales efforts are directed to the smallest possible niche audience. By doing so, you are able to create a strong market-to-message match. This means that your prospective client is reminded of themselves by your communication. By zeroing in on a very focused audience, you significantly increase the likelihood that your message will shine through the clutter.

Thus, it's worthwhile to take some time and think through what an ideal client is for your business. This exercise begins with a series of questions:

- Who has the strongest desire for what you do or know?
- Who could spend the most money for what you do or know?
- Who would make the most money from what you do or know?
- Who are you most passionate about serving?
- Have they demonstrated a willingness to spend money on your type of product or service?
- Are they easy to reach?

Sometimes your niche market shifts over time. According to interior designer Melonie Nottingham:

> I began working primarily with divorced women who were starting over in life. Over time, I started to get inquiries from their lawyers. This developed into a secondary niche in which I worked with many family law attorneys. The two groups were symbiotic in the sense that each referred great clients to me.

You'll have more success in marketing to a niche if you develop a story that explains why you're focusing on it. The most compelling stories you can tell are those that demonstrate your track record of success in a particular niche. You express that "I've helped others just like you to (achieve a goal or solve a problem) thanks to my in-depth understanding of (something)." This is a very compelling marketing flag to wave, and it tends to get a lot of attention.

One concrete reason for focusing on a particular niche is that you have relevant professional experience. For example, Samuel Maxwell specializes in fractional jet-leasing programs. He previously worked for Gulfstream Aerospace as an engineer, so he has a great story and a wealth of knowledge about the field. Similarly, financial advisor Setu Mazumdar specializes in work with physicians, and he is an MD himself, which gives him a level of credibility that most others in his niche do not have. In other cases, perhaps a family member or friend involved in a particular niche needed help with an issue. You were able to help, they told you how invaluable you had been, and you decided to assist other people with the same type of issue.

Yet another common way to engage with a niche is to reapply lessons learned elsewhere. This approach can be presented as: "The problem with the ABC industry is that everyone is doing the exact same thing. I've worked in twenty-four different niche businesses, and I can apply the best practices from outside of your industry to make you successful." Business consultant Jay Abraham has built a highly successful practice this way. By positioning himself as having worked in dozens of different niches, Jay does a masterful job of communicating that his broad perspective is a compelling reason to engage with him.

This discussion is about how to market your business. We want to identify the most effective way to get affluent clients to pay attention to you. It's a fact that a highly targeted niche marketing message will beat out a general message to a broad market every time. We therefore want to identify the right niches for you.

I'm not suggesting that your entire business needs to be focused on just one niche. The important point is that you need to have a compelling reason to focus on a particular group. When viewed as a whole, you may notice that your clientele comes from many different niches. Over time, you may have multiple marketing campaigns, and each might be directed at a particular niche audience.

In addition to having an ideal client and a backstory in mind, you might consider a number of additional factors when working to identify your ideal client niche. The first is market size. You could choose a pond in which there are a lot of fish, but the banks will be filled with competing fishermen. You could instead choose a pond in which there are few fish, and you'd have fewer anglers along the bank. There are many tradeoffs to consider, but one key point is to make sure to know the size of the market before jumping in. You don't want to look back a year down the road and realize that the market isn't as big as you had thought.

Market size should factor into your decision, but it shouldn't be the only point you consider. The truth is that you can still make a lot of money by focusing on even a very small niche. Conversely, you can have great difficulty gaining entry into a large niche, especially if there are a number of large, established players.

Another major factor to consider is the difficulty of reaching your prospects. You want to focus on niches in which you can target the prospective clients. Are there magazines or blogs dedicated to the market you are targeting? Are there relevant associations? Are there other people selling products or services to this group that you could potentially create a joint venture with? Note that reachability can be an issue if you try to define a niche through attitudes or behaviors. For example, don't say "I market to people who are seeking greater fulfillment in their lives." It's tough to find those people.

Sometimes geography is an important factor, but sometimes it's not. You need to figure out whether meeting people face to face is actually important for your business. Would you be happier doing business with people you could sit across from, or would you be just as comfortable communicating with them by phone and email? It's important that you check your assumptions. You may think that you need to interface with clients in person when you actually don't.

One way of making your niche laser-focused is to target a single gender. I work with a female financial advisor who originally focused on retirees. That's a tough market with lots of competition. She changed her niche to widows because, as a widow herself, she has a natural empathy for this audience. She also has a story to tell that lets them know that she understands them better than any of her competition.

You also want to make sure that you are targeting the right buyer. Selling expensive products to students doesn't make sense, but selling to their parents does. An example of this is a company called Ad Zoo. Their niche market consists of creative types who haven't settled on a career and who don't want a typical job. For $45,000, they offer a two-year training program for becoming a copywriter or graphic artist. The cost is well beyond the reach of young adults without stable employment, but their parents are often able and willing to foot the bill, so the marketing is directed at them.

Yet another niche-related factor to consider is competition. How much competition is there in your niche? Ironically, having no competition is a big red flag that says a lot about the viability of the niche. None of us are so smart that we're the first ones to think about selling something to a particular group of people. It's very rare that what you're offering hasn't been offered before. A lack of competition may mean that there's not much hunger for it or that it's available for free on the internet.

Ideally, what you want is bad competition. You hope to find enough competitors to make you feel good about the viability of the niche, but you want to see that they're doing a lousy job at marketing their products or services. If there's intense competition in a niche, and if the competition seems to be doing a good job of marketing, you'll need to ask, "What can I offer that others can't? Is there some unique way I can position my products or services?" If you can't come up with reasonable answers, you might want to think about a different niche.

The classic twin levers for motivating people to buy something are pain and gain. Either the customer wants to avoid pain or get out of pain they're currently experiencing or they want to achieve some sort of gain. Both of these levers are important, but they tend to be used in different stages of the client-attraction process. Pain tends to be the most effective for getting people's initial attention. Of course, we will need to show our prospects that they can achieve the desired gain before they'll give us money, but the pain is what will hook them initially.

Closely related to pain is fear. If we can communicate a message that focuses on the fear of some pain that might occur, we're likely to get a lot of people interested in what we have to offer. As one of my marketing professors said, "It's easier to sell fear than it is prevention."

You may have heard the term "Unique Selling Proposition" (USP). The notion of USP was developed in the 1940s by advertising executive Rosser Reeves of Ted Bates & Company. Many business owners feel pressure to develop their USP, but most of their efforts amount to little more than an exercise in frustration. This is because, for most of us, there just isn't anything truly unique about what we do.

However, you may be able to combine elements of what you do to create a service that others in your niche are not offering. For example, I discovered that while the advice I was providing was helpful, the real need was for implementation. As I analyzed this, it made perfect sense. My clients tend to spend the majority of their day delivering their services. They simply don't have the additional time or energy that's necessary to implement a marketing program.

Eventually, the proverbial light bulb went on and led me to offer done-for-you marketing programs. Now I had two advantages: 1) I focused on a marketing system rather than just a single activity, and 2) I offered a service in which we actually do the work. Is this truly unique? No, not really. Many other marketing consultants offer the same scope and services, but none of them were playing in my niche.

Note how useful it was for me to know my competition. This is one of the reasons to subscribe to all of your competitors' newsletters and mailing lists, even if they serve niches other than yours. There may be something they're doing that you can transplant into your niche to give yourself a unique advantage.

With all that we've just covered, you are now ready to create your ideal client avatar. This in turn will enable you to create marketing and sales messages that break through the nose and clutter. As we've discussed, this is particularly important when focusing on affluent prospects.

Let's begin with a quick exercise that I first learned from marketer Frank Kern. Answering the questions below will help you identify the perfect prospect for what you are selling. It will also help you get into the mindset of your niche audience. Note that you should write down what immediately comes to mind. It's not meant to be an analytical exercise.

John (or Jane) is my ideal client. S/he is ________ years old.

His/her three biggest frustrations are:

1.
2.
3.

Sometimes s/he even wakes up in the middle of the night worrying about ________________.

If s/he could wave a magic wand, s/he would want the these three things to occur:

1.
2.
3.

When s/he goes online to find a potential answer to this problem, s/he may enter keywords into Google such as:

1.
2.
3.

If s/he is going to do business with me, s/he needs to believe I can do three things:

1.
2.
3.

The myth s/he believes (which I will shatter) is __________.

S/he might not invest in my products or services because:

1.
2.
3.

The biggest obstacle s/he faces when trying to solve this problem is ________________.

It's very important that you complete this exercise before moving ahead to the implementation of the marketing strategy. The competition for the affluent market is extremely intense. The clearer your visualization of your ideal client is, the more effective your client-attraction strategy will be.

Chapter 2:
Let's focus on you

2.1 What you need–the basics

Now that we've taken a look at the affluent as a group, let's shift our focus onto you. What's it going to take for you to be successful with the very wealthy? First and foremost, you're going to need to be willing to work very hard. Most everyone says they're willing, but the reality is that the energy and commitment dissipates rather quickly for most people. It's easy to get excited about something. The real challenge is to stay excited.

The reality is that there are a lot of things that are outside of your control, but how hard you work is not one of them. The world is a competitive place. There are a lot of other people who want to do business with precisely the same wealthy clients that you do. They are as unlikely to have a natural connection with that person as you are, so you are both starting from the same point. Which of you is going to win?

The most likely to win is the person who doesn't give up. It's the person who is willing to make one more call and send one more email, who is willing to take time to think about "What am I overlooking that might enable me to build a relationship with this person?" Mark Cuban says that success in any business activity depends upon your "willingness to outwork and outlearn everyone." The person who does that is most likely to win.

What else are you going to need? You'll need ambition. You have to *want* success. I know this seems a bit obvious, and if you ask 100 people if they desire success, you can bet that pretty much all of them will say that they do. There's a huge difference, though, between saying you want success and having the intestinal fortitude to *really* go after it.

Why do so many people fail to achieve the success they say they desire? There are probably a few reasons, but one of the huge ones is that they get discouraged. They just aren't able to overcome or deal with the negatives they hear whenever they set out on one of life's journeys.

Sylvester Stallone describes the needed tenacity as an "alligator hide." You have to be able to take the criticism. You have to be able to put blinders on and forge ahead even when everyone you know, even the people who love you the most, tells you that you're just plain crazy, foolish or dumb to try to do what you aspire to do. That's one of the reasons why motivational videos, books, mentors, and coaches are important. Remaining motivated is perhaps one of the toughest challenges we all face.

A personal case in point is my writing. This is my ninth book. I've written books that have been very successful, but I've also written books that only sold where my closest relatives live. I try to write something every day. Some days I can write a lot, and other days I can barely get three paragraphs written. What's discouraging is to read over what I wrote the day before and realize that it isn't very good or is, in fact, just plain bad. It's at those times that self-doubt creeps in. I ask myself why I'm doing this. After all, after thirty years, I don't *need* to do this.

But that's not entirely true. Perhaps I don't need to write another book from a financial perspective, but I do need to do so for what is probably a more compelling reason. Legendary Notre Dame football coach Lew Holz says, "You need three things in life. You need something to do. You need someone to love. You need something to hope for and look forward to."

Sure, it's discouraging to spend an hour or three writing something only to later realize that it's mostly a bunch of crap. It's discouraging to throw it out and realize that you need to start over, but that's the process. It's true whether you're writing a book, putting a marketing campaign in place, or following up with that person who seemed so interested in you when you first met but who now ghosts you.

I often use the metaphor of learning to juggle. A lot of potential discouragement awaits in any venture that's worth doing. Interestingly, that discouragement can work in your favor, because most people simply give up. They'll try one thing, and if it doesn't work, they'll give up on the entire project.

You don't want to just try one thing in an attempt to be successful, though. In over thirty years, I've never met a successful person who relied on just one method for building relationships with the affluent. Sure, at some point in time that person may end up getting the majority of their clients through word of mouth and referrals. If you dig a little bit deeper, however, you'd notice that there are books, podcasts, social media posts, and a host of other things that are driving those referrals.

Especially when you're starting out, it's a fool's errand to rely on referrals for all your business. At this stage, you simply don't know enough wealthy people. I often think that people hide behind "All my business comes from word of mouth and referral" because they are either too scared or lack the necessary knowledge and willingness to market themselves.

"Don't overlook the importance of self-confidence," advises interior designer Shauna Levinson. Her clients typically spend over one million dollars for her home-decorating services in Palm Beach, New York and Los Angeles. She says:

> No one wants to admit that they're lacking in self-confidence, especially to others. However, it's very common, especially when you're starting out, to feel hesitant when trying to engage with someone who is older, richer and more successful than you. However, you'll need to at least appear self confident even if your palms are sweating if you're going to be successful at developing relationships with the wealthy.

So how do you do that? Harry Greenberg is a private jet broker and manages a team of six junior brokers. He says:

> I'm the guy at the firm who developed a reputation for taking younger people and successfully preparing them for working with very wealthy clients. One of the most common questions they ask me is "What do I talk about with these prospective clients? After all, I'm considerably younger than they are and haven't (yet) achieved the level of success or wealth they have." It's a real issue, and my advice to them is twofold. First, have a range of interests. Be able to talk about a variety of topics. Then, there should be one or two that you know in depth.

People tend to be interested in those who have a passion. As Tom Ford once commented, "The problem with most social gatherings is that at the end of the evening you don't know anything new." People who can share their passion in a way that makes it fun for those who know little or nothing about the topic are remembered positively. Naturally, you need to be able to read your audience. Sometimes your passion for making homemade honey will be of interest, but other times, not so much. You also need to be able to talk about your passion in a way so that doesn't come across as a lecture. There's a real art to this.

If you want to be conversant about a variety of topics, you need to consume information from diverse sources. Most people only focus their attention on local crime, sports and politics. While sports can be a good opening topic, avoid the other two. And, please, for the love of God, don't talk about the weather. If nothing else, it sends the message that you have absolutely nothing of interest to impart.

Burt Sansifor decided to expand the marketing of his high-end educational consulting practice to include women. He realized that he needed to broaden his base of knowledge about topics that the tribe of affluent and successful women discuss. He recalls:

> Although many of them were extremely successful businesswomen, they also had great interest in fashion, interior design and spirituality. I found that by adding Town & Country, Vogue and Good Housekeeping to my reading list, I was able to engage in conversations I otherwise wouldn't have been able to.

Beyond having a wide variety of topics that you have at least a passing knowledge about, the most important skill, the one that will make you more interesting to virtually anyone, is the ability to ask good questions. If you're starting out, the best piece of advice that ultra-luxury broker Jon Grauman offers is to "Embrace your newness." One of the most effective ways to do that while at the same time impressing the affluent individual you're speaking with is to use questions.

If you develop only one skill in your pursuit of building relationships with the wealthy, the ability to ask good questions is the one you need. This skill is partly attitudinal and partly tactical. The tactical part is arguably the easier.

Most everyone who is a good conversationalist has a list of

questions to draw from. For example:

- What's been the highlight of your day thus far?
- How do you know the people here?
- How did you decide on that as a career? (This is the follow-up question to "What do you do for a living?")
- What did you want to be when you were a kid? (This is a follow up question to the previous one.)
- Do you collect anything?
- Someone recently asked me, "If you didn't know how old you are, how old would you think you are?" How would you answer that?

It's also useful to have a ready list of follow-up questions such as:

- What's an example of that?
- Why do you say that?
- What would be an alternative?
- What does (a term they used) mean?

Regarding that last follow-up question, when someone uses a term we are unfamiliar with, we far too often let it slide under the assumption that it will make us seem ignorant or unsophisticated. Ironically, the exact opposite is true. Most people love to talk and educate, and this question stimulates that desire.

In general, it's good to have a few questions prepared since most people are terrible conversationalists. You ask a question, then they answer and wait patiently for you to ask another. Why people can't just ask the same question they just answered is beyond me. However, we have to deal with the world the way it is, not the way we wish it would be.

In case you need them, there are a few general questions that people typically enjoy answering. They can be great when there's a lull in the conversation. Examples of such questions are: Are you a cat or dog person? What's your favorite breakfast? What's the best restaurant you've eaten at this month?

The other requirement for being a good conversationalist is to fine-tune your attitude. Specifically, you want to be curious. My dad, even at the age of eighty-nine, remained an intensely curious person. As he told me once, "The real trick for not acting old is to be curious about a lot of different things. I don't know how many times I didn't think the topic would be interesting, but by the end of the conversation, I realized I had learned a lot, and that it was in fact pretty fascinating."

Unfortunately, most people approach conversations with the intention of talking and then waiting to talk. If you do that, it's really hard to figure out what questions to ask. However, if you allow your curiosity to guide you, questions will be natural and spontaneous. Those in sales have an innate advantage since they've been trained how to ask questions. We all could benefit from attending such a training program.

While preparation and curiosity are valuable tools, one of the biggest challenges is entering a conversation that's already in progress. First, you need to read your audience. If it is apparent that they are engaged in a serious discussion, move on. However, if it appears to be a social conversation, a good strategy is to position yourself slightly behind the shoulder of the person being spoken to. That way you're in the speaker's eye-line.

If the speaker has any social skills at all, when they reach a natural break in their sentence, they will acknowledge you, usually with a polite "Hello." The easiest thing to say at this point is "So, what are we talking about?" This question displays good manners and enables you to seamlessly enter the conversation.

If you're uncomfortable approaching groups of people, another option is to position yourself in a location that people are headed toward. I learned this trick back in high school as a way to deal with my discomfort socializing at parties. I would perch myself next to the refrigerator or wherever the beer was kept. A variation on this technique works just as well today. Just stand by the food or the bar.

Simply standing in line enables you to strike up a conversation with the person either behind or in front of you. A wealth management client of mine swears by the effectiveness of this method. He'll stand in line for a drink, strike up some conversations, and then go to the end of the line and repeat the exercise.

Another effective way to build self-confidence in social situations is to work as a part of a team. There's a lot of benefit to going to networking events or sales calls with one or two other people, and Frank Guiffre, Managing Director at Kourtney Van Patten, encourages his team members as follows:

> The beauty of going with another person is that it significantly reduces the awkwardness that we all face in these networking situations. It's likely that the two of you will have different interests, so it doubles the likelihood that, as a team, you'll find some common ground with the person with whom you're speaking.
>
> Another benefit–and this really helps with self-confidence–is that at the end of the conversation, when the person walks away, you're not standing there alone. That totally sucks. Rather, the two of you can decide where to go. When you do this with a partner, it's a lot less nerve racking to initiate conversations.

Do extroverts have a considerable advantage when it comes to being confident in social situations? Can introverts be successful in networking events? Sally Clarkberg, managing director for an international insurance brokerage, claims that both introverts and extroverts can be successful. She says:

> One would think that extroverts would naturally be better in social situations, but that's not necessarily true. First, I'm not a believer that there are total introverts or complete extroverts. I think most of us are a blend. We tend to be extroverted when we're

> comfortable and introverted in new or unfamiliar situations.
>
> While extroverts tend to be more comfortable around people, we've had a number of instances in which they came across as cocky. They also tend not to listen particularly well, which is the proverbial kiss of death when working with the affluent. I've had to coach the extroverts on my team to talk less and listen more.
>
> In some ways, it's actually easier to develop introverts. Their natural default position is to listen, which is great. Where they need help is on what types of questions to ask and how to keep the conversation moving along. One thing I tell them that really helps with their self esteem is to remember that this is not a sales presentation. You're not tasked with trying to sell anyone anything. In fact I don't want them selling.
>
> The purpose of these interactions is to start the relationship process. That's it. Once they realize that the pressure is off, if they're equipped with a laundry list of questions to ask when things get slow, they usually do fine.

Feedback is a crucial component when developing the confidence and social skills that are necessary for success. Josh Battle, whose firm manages concierge medical spas, adds this about building self-confidence:

> Of course, as a leader in the company, it's also my job to make sure that team members, especially the younger ones, get positive feedback. You want to make sure they know that you believe in them and will do everything you can to help them be successful. That doesn't mean that you don't engage in frank feedback and tough love on occasion, but if the underlying message is one of support, it's amazing the positive impact that has on self-confidence.

A classic piece of advice that's often heard but terribly difficult to follow is to simply be yourself. The more comfortable, casual and natural you are, the better you will come across. Confidence also comes as a byproduct of desire. If you really want to work with the affluent, and if you have a deep, burning desire to be successful, it will motivate you to do the things that are necessary but that you might avoid if you were less committed.

Not everyone thinks that simply being yourself is a particularly effective strategy, however. Leo Flint runs a wealth advisory firm that caters to professional athletes and entertainers. He argues:

> I think that just trying to be yourself is terrible advice, especially when you are starting out. The "yourself" is a person who's uncomfortable, shy, and awkward around famous and successful people. Why would you want to be that person?
>
> I think what you want to be is a version of your-

> self. Observe the people who are successful i
> firm, and emulate those characteristics that y
> mire. Some of them will fit with your own personality and others won't. Cherry pick the ones that do, and create a mosaic of characteristics.
>
> I know it sounds silly, but when I was starting out, I'd look at myself in the mirror before going to an event or client meeting. I'd mentally adopt this character of the person I planned on playing. Now the key is that your alter ego can't be dramatically different from how you are in real life. It's more of an enhanced version. I'll admit that I felt a bit uncomfortable the first few times I tried this, but eventually, it started to become increasingly natural.

Sarah Henderson manages seven concierge medical practices. The following is her take on self presentation:

> I've found that personal energy and facial expressions are a key for making me feel confident around really wealthy people. This was really driven home when I had three colleagues on three separate occasions ask me "What's wrong?" Apparently, my natural facial expression is a bit of a hang dog, or as my daughter says, a resting bitch face.
>
> Here's a trick I use, which may or may not work for anyone else. I picked it up from Tony Robbins.

> Before I go into a meeting, I go into the restroom and smile into the mirror like some demented comic book villain. What that does is relax and rearrange the muscles in my face into a far more pleasant and happy appearance. Then I throw my shoulders back and exit the restroom at a brisk pace. This is the way that I prime myself for any meeting or event.

2.2 The power of believing in yourself

A lot has been written about the power of believing in yourself, and although it's massively hard to do, there is a very practical reason why believing in yourself is so important. Belief and action are linked. If you don't believe that you can be successful in building affluent relationships, how much effort will you put into it? The obvious answer is "Not much." Sure, you might try a few things, but the likelihood that you'll sustain the effort is very low.

Even more damaging is that this lack of effort will likely produce few results, which will further reduce your level of belief in yourself. This can create a self-perpetuating downward spiral. A lack of belief impedes your willingness to take action, inaction means you get no results, and a lack of results reinforces negative beliefs. The cycle feeds upon itself.

And this brings us back to desire. You have to want this. If you really want something, something that's not a nice-to-have but a must-have, then you take massive action. When you take massive action, you then start to get positive results, and you realize, "Hey this is working. Let's do more of this!" In this case, your brain is working in opposition to the downward spiral. Results give you confidence. Confidence leads to action. Action leads to results. Remember, though, that you need to by taking the right type of action. A salesman can knock on 100 doors, but it's a waste of effort if his pitch is "You don't want this, do you?"

I'll be talking about the specific strategies you can use to build relationships with the wealthy in subsequent chapters, but I cannot overemphasize the importance of mindset and confidence. So, how do we flip the switch and increase the level of confidence we need in order to be successful? The key is to shift your focus.

Tom Stillwater is an estate planning attorney. Although he is a young-looking thirty-four year old, his typical client is in their early fifties. He says:

> One of the problems I faced early on was that I both *was* young and *looked* young. I thought that because of that, potential clients wouldn't take me seriously. Since that was my mindset, guess what? They didn't take me seriously. Attitude affects everything.
>
> Now I can't tell you that all of a sudden one day my self consciousness about being young went away by magic. However, a couple of things really helped me. When I was starting out, I'd ask older lawyers how they got clients, and they all told me it was referrals and word of mouth. That's great when you're established, but it isn't particularly helpful when you're at the beginning of your career.

> Although I was self conscious about how I looked, I started to notice that if someone met me after they had read my articles or white papers, they didn't seem terribly concerned about my age. That was a bit of an ah-ha moment and made me realize that leveraging my writing skills would really pay dividends. Instead of just going to networking events, I really focused on how I could get more visibility for what I was writing.
>
> The second piece of the puzzle was that I developed a marketing plan to do just that, and more importantly, I actually implemented it. I was absolutely amazed that out of the group of twenty-five people in the mastermind coaching program I joined, only one or two of us completed the assignments.
>
> Having a marketing plan in place that focused on using my articles as a method for getting attention did wonders for my self-confidence. I found that when I actually talked with a prospective client, I was a lot more self-confident, which led to attracting a lot more new affluent clients.

Tom's ah-ha moment arrived when he realized that his articles gave him credibility and confidence. There will be a similar moment in which you will come to believe that what you want to achieve is possible. Commitment, hard work, perseverance, and no small measure of faith are necessary to get you to that point, but once you reach that point, the world changes. Your success might not be consistent yet or at the level you want, but from that moment on, you will now know that it's possible.

We are always learning, trying, failing and succeeding. That doesn't change. What does change is the belief we have in ourselves once we experience that ah-ha moment. Arguably, the hardest part is getting yourself to that point. After that, it's mostly a matter of strategy and implementation. Certainly, things can still go terribly wrong, but having experienced that moment, you'll have the motivation to push through when inevitably faced with periodic setbacks.

Somewhat ironically, developing motivation when your back is against the wall is easier than it is when the task in front of you is something that you would like to but don't have to do. For example, without the proverbial gun to your head, it can be easy to blow off the art gallery networking opportunity and tell yourself that you'll go next time. Regarding the skillful use of pressure, financial planner Stacey Enbright says:

> Chunk it down. Don't say, "I'm going to go to all these events, join all these groups, write all these articles." It's exhausting, and you'll wind up not doing any of them. If you have nine different things you "could" do, then there's no pressure on you to actually do one of them. It's better to select one, and say to yourself, "This is what I'm going to focus on doing next week." The more commitment, the more effort and better results.

Clearly, there are a lot of different ways to improve your self-confidence. Personally, I'm a huge fan of motivational books, videos and podcasts, but I also recognize their limitations. Their effects don't last. You constantly have to find ways to re-motivate yourself. One of my clients described his approach as follows:

> Something I found extremely helpful in building up my confidence was changing my perspective. I would take time each morning to visualize what my life would be like if I was successful in cultivating relationships with these wealthy people. I imagined how interesting my life would be if I was interacting on a regular basis with people who were so successful.
>
> By shifting my focus from worrying that people would ignore me and find me boring, I focused on what life would be like when I had these relationships. I found my stress level went down, my anxiety went down, and my confidence increased.

What I ultimately recommend is that you try a lot of different things and see what works for you. For me and for my most successful clients, faith and purpose have built and sustained self-confidence more than anything else. I don't mean faith in a religious sense, but I'm referring to a belief that what you are doing will ultimately get you what you want. For example, you want to have faith that by going to events and continuing to meet people, you will eventually have the type of business and the kind of life that you most desire.

While faith will help you maintain the right attitude, a sense of purpose will keep you driven and motivated to take action. Purpose enables you to overcome shyness, a lack of self-confidence, and pretty much any other obstacle that might stand in your way. Purpose is powerful, but it must be true to you. To succeed with affluent marketing, it is crucially important that building relationships and doing business with the wealthy are very important to you.

2.3 Appearances

Let's move onto the next topic on the agenda: appearances. We all make snap judgements. It's not something we're supposed to do, but it's a reality of life. For example, my father associated fat people with a whole host of slovenly behaviors. Were his judgments wrong? Sure, they were wrong some of the time, but they were also right a lot of the time. My wife is much less judgmental than I am, so she's quick to point out that overweight people could be suffering from hormone imbalances, glandular issues, or other issues that are completely out of their control. Yes, but they might instead just be eating too much.

Now, suppose you see a stylish man or woman in a nicely tailored suit. Perhaps they're carrying a designer handbag or wearing an obviously expensive watch. What's the snap judgment you make about that person? Interestingly, it varies enormously, and it depends on your own socio-economic class. A middle-class person will tend to say that they're a snob or unapproachable.

They'd describe them as "not someone I'd like to hang out with." The wealthy, on the other hand, would see this person as one of their own, as part of their tribe.

The point is that you often make snap judgments about people, and they're usually more accurate than not. I think my wife is gradually coming around to my way of thinking. I started to notice it this year when, for our twentieth anniversary, we went to Vegas.

Some people are "Vegas people," but others wouldn't go there if you paid them. I get it, and I pass no judgment. If you haven't been there, it's worth at least one visit if for no other reason than to see what kind of a hotel you can build for $2 billion. It's truly astounding.

As for me, I'm a Vegas guy. Interestingly, I'm not a big gambler, but I love the shows and the architecture. Most of all, I love the people watching in Vegas. The crowd runs the gamut, and you get to see a complete cross section of the American population. This offers some very interesting lessons about tribalism and about how different sects of American society recognize each other and congregate.

Las Vegas hotels run the gamut as well. At the top you have places like the Wynn, Aria and Bellagio. At the bottom you have Harrahs, Bally's, Tropicana and Barbary Coast. In the middle, you have a selection that includes The Mirage, Paris, New York/New York and many others. I'm leaving a lot of them out, but the point is there are hotels and casinos for every different type of person.

One of my favorite people-watching places is the Petrossian Bar located just off the lobby in the Bellagio hotel. They serve drinks along with a choice of caviar, smoked salmon, carpaccio, and other snacks that will put a serious dent in your wallet. It's a great place to watch people. The Bellagio is a very upscale hotel, but it's located in the middle of the Las Vegas strip, which means there is a lot of foot traffic passing through. You see many different types of people from those that obviously belong to those that just as obviously don't.

My wife and I were doing some people-watching in the Petrossian Bar one morning. We first noticed a heavyset lady wearing an oversized green T-shirt featuring Jimmy Buffet. She also sported the requisite fanny pack and well worn Nikes. We next noticed a slender Asian lady with a two-piece ensemble, Gucci bag and shiny heels. She was followed by a fat dude with worn-down sandals who somehow thought that a mumu-style Hawaiian shirt would go well with lime-green cargo shorts. Finally, there was a guy wearing crisp jeans, a polo shirt, a Rolex watch and Pelle loafers.

So tell me, who were the wealthy ones? I know that appearances can be deceiving. Maybe the chunky lady was a real-estate mogul. The Asian woman might have been a hooker. We were in Vegas, after all, so who knows. If I had to place a bet on which of those people had money, though, I would say the guy with the Rolex and loafers and the well-put-together woman.

My Wife Marian is into purses, or *handbags*, rather. (As my friend says, better purses than jewelry...) Marian brought her Chanel bag with her when we went to Vegas, but she also packed another bag with many pockets, and from a utility standpoint, that bag was great for walking around the strip. On our first day out, she wore the pocket-filled tote bag.

The next day, I asked her, "Do you remember when we went shopping at Aria yesterday, and we went into Tom Ford, YSL, and then Prada?"

"Yes," she said.

I continued, "Nobody paid any attention to you. You were invisible."

"True," she said.

"But today at The Forum, you wore your Chanel bag, and we went into Tom Ford, YSL, and Prada. You couldn't take three steps inside the place before some salesperson asked how they could help you."

I had made my point. The truth is that there is a shorthand code that rich people use to identify each other. They look at the bag. They look at the watch. They look at the shoes. There's a uniform. Well, maybe it's not an actual uniform, but there's a look that says, "I'm a part of the tribe." Sure, Zuckerberg can get away with looking like Zuckerberg. However, if you want to get accepted by the wealthy, you probably can't.

I think we can all agree that we live in a far more casual world than we did fifteen years ago. Personally, I think that's both good and bad, but regardless, how a person presents themselves when they leave the house reveals something about them. There are a lot of reasons to care about the way you look, but the most compelling is that looking good makes you feel more confident. As fashion designer Tom Ford said, "A lot of people would really benefit from investing in a full length mirror."

It all starts with taking a look at yourself before you leave the house. What's the look you want? First, it depends on the industry you're in. You need to read the room. Are you working in a high-end art gallery? Then the latest fashions make a lot of sense. Are you working in financial services? Then the latest fashion is likely to cause you problems.

According to a memo sent to employees of J.P. Morgan, "Dressing down when you're talking about money can be easily seen as a sign of disrespect, especially if your clients are older." They further specified that "casual pants, capris, dress and skirts of appropriate length for the workplace" and "business appropriate casual shirts, polo shirts, sweaters, tops and blouses" were allowed under the dress code.

According to Advisor Hub, "Corporate culture filters from the top, and James Dimon's no-tie look is more casual than most financial CEOs." According to *The Wall Street Journal*, after a visit to Silicon Valley, Dimon decided it was time to change the work environment at his bank to match those of more progressive industries. Caveats, of course, came attached. "Business casual is not weekend casual," a memo stressed, and "If you're seeing a client you should dress for that client." The latter clause applied to investment bankers, who are still required to wear suits.

Monica Diaz, a fashion consultant based in New York City, recommends that female investment advisors appear "conservative, polished, current and approachable." She prefers straight dresses with cap, full or three-quarter sleeves that can be worn with or without jackets. Finally, freshly polished quality shoes are equally important for both male and female advisors. Too many advisors pay too little attention to their shoes. That is usually a mistake, because what you wear on your feet has a significant impact on how people view you.

From a general perspective, I want you to think about the word "polished" when it comes to dressing. "Classic with a modern sensibility" is how most well dressed, affluent men would describe their style. Polished looks pricey, but it doesn't have to be. Looking polished means taking time to assess how you look from your hair to the shine of your shoes and everything in between. Very importantly, it also means making sure that your clothes fit you.

If there's one factor that separates the polished from the slobs it's fit. Messy is the antithesis of polished. Messy screams middle or lower class. Unfortunately, it's the default style for far too many people. As Roger Thomas, head of design for Wynn Resorts said, "People tend to take on the characteristics of a room. They feel glamorous in a glamorous space and rich in a rich space." I think the same is true for how you dress.

You need to assess how you look in a brutally honest and architectural manner. What colors and styles look best on you? If you dress well, you'll feel more confident, which will improve your ability to interact and develop relationships with the wealthy. The more what you wear makes you feel good, the more it will enhance your life and reduce stress. The real key is to find something that works for you.

2.4 Creating your personal brand

Let's talk now about your brand and, specifically, about how to create one that will attract more wealthy clients. Developing your brand starts with identifying exactly who you are trying to attract. Remember, the affluent are not just a single market. They break down into numerous sub-niches based on things like gender, age, and how they acquired their money.

The extent to which you sub-niche your business depends on a couple of factors. For example, I live in Pinehurst, NC in a golf-resort community of about 18,000. There's a fair amount of wealth here, but since this is a small community, that doesn't necessarily mean that there are a lot of wealthy people. If you have a local business here, subdividing the affluent population wouldn't make a lot of sense. In contrast, if you market nationally or internationally, you may find that you get more attention and traction if you focus on a niche or niches within the affluent community.

It's important to keep in mind that what I'm talking about is strictly for marketing purposes. A sub-niche does not need to represent your entire business. It's relatively easy to create parallel marketing initiatives with websites and marketing collateral that focus on individual niches. In my experience, the record was set by a client who had nineteen separate marketing funnels directed at various subsets of the affluent market. That's probably a bit excessive, but I will admit that it worked extremely well.

The point is that the more that you narrow your focus, the more effective your efforts will be. We want to optimize the *message-to-market match*, which is the extent to which your target audience sees a reflection of itself in your marketing materials. This is important for any marketing initiative, but it's particularly important if you're focused on attracting more wealthy clients.

"Branding" is really just another word for describing your attention-getting strategy. How are you going to stand out in the crowd? How are you differentiating yourself from your competition? Again, just remember to pause and think about *whom* you want the attention from. The more you target your brand message, the more likely it is that it will resonate with the people you want to attract.

Your brand message is a single sentence that guides all of your marketing activity, and establishing it is the first step in developing your personal brand. This step is fundamental to your overall branding efforts, and it's deceptively simple. In fact, it's so simple that many companies and individuals gloss over it and move on to implementation. That's a mistake.

I suggest using a format that makes your brand message memorable, that enables you to refer back to it easily, and that ensures that all of your efforts can be aligned to it. To develop your brand message, complete the following sentence: We help (niche audience) (solve or achieve) (what type of problem or what type of goal). That's it! Take a moment to write out your brand message.

Now that you've established it, we can take further steps to bring it to life. We're going to focus on three elements: image, story and personality. Let's start with image, which covers a lot of ground. It includes the look and feel of your marketing materials, your personal appearance, the look of your office, and the culture of your team.

When most of us think of the word "brand," logos and imagery immediately come to mind. There's no doubt that these can play a significant role. Mauricio Umansky, CEO of luxury real estate firm The Agency, credits part of their early success in the hyper-competitive Los Angeles market to their distinctive logo. She says, "It conveyed an image of contemporary luxury that was completely in sync with how we wanted to position the agency."

You'll also have to choose colors for your website, social channels and marketing collateral. Amy Sinclair, a financial advisor to the affluent, describes her selection process:

> Green was my first choice, but as I researched what other advisors were doing, it seemed like I'd get lost in the crowd. Also, the connection between green and money was a bit too obvious. A color consultant I hired suggested combining green with black or gold. Black in particular creates an image of strength and authority. Gold signifies wealth and stability. I also considered blue, which is associated with trust and conveys a more youthful and modern image. However, since most of my clients are older, I settled on the green/black/gold color palate.

If you're focused on marketing to women, you'll want your image to be softer and more romantic. While I would probably stay away from pink, muted green and lavender tones can be extremely effective for building a brand message of trust and accessibility.

Next up, let's discuss the role that personal style and appearance play in your brand. As Deion Sanders says, "Look good, play good. Play good, get paid good." There's a lot of truth to that.

Obviously you need to dress for the occasion and the audience. The person who runs a high-end art gallery should have a different personal style than a wealth manager. Raymond Parker, who sells leasing programs for private jets, says:

> How you dress has little or nothing to do with you. It has everything to do with the person that you're meeting. First impressions are everything, and if you're not careful, your first impression can also be your last. It's worth the time and effort to meet with a styling consultant to get a sense for what colors work best on you. It's very true that the rich will make snap judgments about you which are largely based on what you are wearing.

For many people, interacting with the very wealthy can be intimidating, especially if they are considerably older and wealthier than you. Looking sharp not only compliments your brand but also gives you a boost of confidence. This also ties into the personality component of branding that I'll discuss shortly.

Note that your brand also extends to your work environment. What's the feeling one gets when they enter your office? What are the chairs like in the waiting area? What type of art is hanging on the walls? It's important to purposefully consider how you want the environment to make visitors feel.

Regardless of what type of business you are in, it can be useful to visit high-end retailers to study how the atmosphere is created. Designers like Gucci, Prada, Tom Ford, Ralph Lauren, and YSL each present a unique brand image. During our recent visit to Las Vegas, my wife and I took time to visit many of these high end designers' retail facilities in the Aria Plaza. As I looked around, I reflected on how the interior design made me feel. As architect and designer Roger Thomas has said, "People tend to take on the characteristics of a room. They feel glamorous in a glamorous space and rich in a rich space."

Your brand is also linked inextricably to the culture of your business. A great case study to examine is that of Dr. A., one of my clients. By all accounts, she is a very successful dermatologist. She's well educated and personable, and after ten years in business, she decided that she wanted to focus her practice on cosmetic dermatology. Many dermatologists have the same practice focus, and it presents well known challenges. One challenge is that botox, fillers, liposuction and other cosmetic procedures are rarely covered by insurance. Since the patient pays for them out of pocket, the client needs to have a large amount of discretionary income.

Even when you know who you need to market to, these services can be difficult to market effectively because they are somewhat commoditized. For example, botox injections are offered by ophthalmologists, nurse practitioners, estheticians and others. Dr. A did an exemplary job by communicating the artistry associated with cosmetic fillers. Very astutely, her marketing contained just a dusting of fear about what one could look like if the work wasn't performed by a true professional dedicated to the practice.

While her numerous videos and other marketing efforts brought prospective patients to her practice, the conversion rate was surprisingly low, especially among the most affluent of her prospects. We identified that the problem was the culture of her business. Once you were ushered from the waiting room to the treatment area, the feeling was similar to entering a five-star spa. The nurses and medical technicians tended to all your needs. You were made to feel cared for. The overarching message was that everyone was absolutely delighted that you had selected them for your treatment. The problem, however, was that you had to get into the treatment area to experience that level of service.

When you first entered the business, the staff was brusque and cold. Even more problematic for impression forming was a similarly gruff exit. First impressions matter a lot, but how you are made to feel as you pay your bill and leave the premises determines your overall feeling about a place. The experience of the facility was reminiscent of that of a busy urban emergency room. In fact, this was where many of the staff were from.

Dr. A had a clear vision for what her brand was, but she had failed to train the front office staff accordingly. It was absolutely killing her business. The good news was that once this was identified, it was relatively easy to train the staff on how to more effectively interact with patients. As marketing consultant Dan Kenney says, "Small hinges swing large doors." Something as simple as how clients are greeted or how they are treated as they settle their accounts can be very important. The brand experience needs to be consistent, and everyone that interacts with clients needs to exhibit the same level of customer service.

Additional aspects of image will be mentioned in relation to specific selling techniques addressed in Chapter 4, but having covered the basics of image, let's move on to stories, which constitute the second element of your personal brand. Why are stories so important? Because people don't remember facts and figures. They remember stories. Stories help you break away from the pack, and they play a huge role in helping you become a recognized expert in your field.

You want to focus on two different types of stories: stories about you, and stories about your business, products or services. Let's start with the story about you, which is often referred to as your "origin story." You'll find that this is particularly important for building relationships with the wealthy.

Consider the experience of Dr. Matt Trainer, a cosmetic dentist with a very wealthy clientele:

> What's interesting is that so many of my clients are self-made success stories and come from very modest backgrounds. I've found that they connect with me when they learn of my background growing up in foster homes and attending both undergraduate and graduate schools on scholarships. They relate to this up-from-the-bootstraps background that we share.

This doesn't mean that if you don't have a rags-to-riches backstory you need to invent one. The key to an effective origin story is that it be authentic to you. That's how you connect with prospective clients. Connection is the key to likeability, which is an often overlooked component in your branding strategy.

People want to do business with people they like. Sure, you may go to the cranial surgeon with absolutely no bedside manner because he is the best in the world, but the reality is that for most of us, people can go elsewhere. They'll do business with those that they feel most comfortable with. That's really the purpose of your origin story.

An effective way to create this story is to model it after the Hero's Journey. This is a common story template first popularized by literature professor Joseph Campbell in his book *The Hero with a Thousand Faces*. George Lucas credits Campbell with influencing his creation of the Star Wars movies, and the Hero's Journey reflects the underlying structure in everything from Spiderman to Harry Potter.

The storyline has three main sections. In the first, the hero is compelled to leave the world they're in. This change could be due to an interaction with another person, or it might result from a realization that success requires making a change. As an example, consider the story of yacht broker Harrison Ward:

> My dream growing up was to be a professional actor, and I gave it a good shot. Unfortunately, as much as I loved being an actor, all the stuff that you

> have to subject yourself to in order to get the roles left me frustrated and depressed. I used to go for long walks down the beach and found that I was increasingly drawn to the beautiful boats I saw in the Los Angeles harbor. I've always loved nautical architecture and interior design, so I would sit for hours just staring at the boats, comparing one to another.
>
> One day, as I was sitting and gazing at the boats, an older gentleman came down the gangway and walked purposefully over to where I was sitting. My initial reaction was that I was in trouble and he was coming over to scare me away. Instead, he said that he had been watching me watch the boats for the past few weeks and wondered if I might be interested in taking a tour of one of them.
>
> It turns out he ran a very successful yacht leasing company. I didn't know I was at a job interview (although I later learned that I sort of was), and I just let my curiosity and enthusiasm to actually tour one of these magnificent boats come through. Suffice it to say I wound up going to work for him, and the direction of my life changed completely.

The second stage in the Hero's Journey is the Initiation. The hero embarks on their adventure, but it's not all kittens and rainbows. The new reality is more difficult than anticipated, but by using skills developed earlier in life, the hero overcomes the obstacles. Harrison Ward describes his experience in this stage as follows:

> Although I absolutely loved the boats, I wasn't anticipating that I was going to be in sales. I'd never sold anything in my life, and to be perfectly frank, I viewed sales people as a lower form of humanity. A big part of the job is taking prospective clients on tours of the yacht. My presentation consisted of telling the guest that this was a door, this was a window, and if you looked out in the distance, you would see water. I'm still amazed that I didn't get fired in my first month.
>
> However, there was something about the whole yacht world that just resonated with me. I loved the boats, but I was also intrigued with the type of person who would consider shelling out hundreds of thousands of dollars to lease one. These people also intimidated the crap out of me, which is why I probably was so terrible at my job. I really struggled with my shyness and the fact that everyone I spoke with was a lot wealthier and older than me.
>
> I struggled until I discovered that the solution to my discomfort was within me. I had been a decent actor. I just hated auditioning. There is a lot of truth to why it's called a "cattle call." However, it dawned on me that if "Harrison" was intimidated by all these rich

> people, the character of "Harrison Super Star Yacht Broker" wasn't. I'd never actually call myself that out loud, but that was the persona I created. Once I did that, my world changed. I was a lot more confident, a lot more relaxed, and ultimately a lot more successful. My shyness and discomfort about being around the super wealthy went away.

The third part of the Hero's Journey is the Return, which is the culmination of the hero's adventure. We'll again take our example from Harrison Ward:

> I was doing well. After about a year, I found that I was now really comfortable around wealthy people. My commissions grew, and I was actually able to afford to buy the condo I was renting. Life was going really well, but I realized that long term, I didn't want to be just an employee. I wanted to have a business of my own. I felt that I owed a real debt of gratitude to my mentor, so I didn't want to just quit and set up a competitive shop.
>
> As luck would have it, due to some family issues, he decided to move from Los Angeles to Miami and offered me the opportunity to buy the business. That was super exciting, but I'll admit that a lot of the old doubts started to resurface. It's one thing to be an individual contributor. It's completely different when

> you're an owner.
>
> But I knew deep down that this is the path I wanted to take. So I made the jump, and now, looking back with the benefit of ten years, I'm so grateful for how my life has turned out. It's amazing to me how chance encounters can lead to new lifelong paths.

The Hero's Journey is a structure that works well for almost any story. Don't feel compelled to follow the structure rigidly, though. Its real purpose is to connect with your prospective client. Since so many of the super wealthy are self made, they identify with someone who has struggled on their journey but persevered.

Clients tell me that they use their origin story in a variety of ways. In social situations, when the inevitable question "So what do you do?" comes up, it's a handy device that enables you to immediately connect with the person you're speaking with.I would also recommend that you incorporate your origin story into your website. Hardly any of the traditional biographies found on websites are memorable, and they certainly don't facilitate a connection with the reader. An origin story addresses these shortcomings.

The second type of brand story you want to tell is about your business, products and services. An illustrative example comes from a small antique store in Atlanta. The owner, Lester Moore, travels the world at the behest of his clients to find unique items for their homes. He often discovers things that aren't right for his clients but that are intriguing nonetheless. He'll purchase them and then offer them for sale in his boutique retail store.

It is well known that everything he offers has a story behind it, and that's his brand. The stories separate his antique store from the countless others in the area. Lester says:

> People love to show off their purchases to their friends. What makes doing that extra fun is to be able to tell a story about a particular item. Everything I sell comes with a great story you can share with your friends.

I happened upon his store a number of years ago and was immediately captivated by a suit of armor he had prominently displayed near the front door. He told me, "Now, to be totally candid with you, this is a replica. It's only about 150 years old, but it was made by the armorers in Seville, Spain. During Medieval times, Seville was the leading maker of armor in the world." He went on to explain that this particular suit of armor would have been worn by the palace guards since it was lighter weight than those typically worn on the battlefield.

The story brought the suit of armor to life, and as I write these words, I'm looking at it in the alcove of my living room. Having the suit of armor is fun, but Lester was completely right: it's equally enjoyable to share its story. Would I have bought it without hearing the story? Perhaps. Once I heard the story, however, my desire to own it increased dramatically.

A few months later I visited the store again, and my eye was caught by a beautiful antique engraved sword. Lester told me:

> Take a look at the name "Robineaux" etched on the scabbard. Legend has it that Monsieur Robineaux, who was the treasurer to Napoleon, was extremely proud of this sword. If you look at it closely, you'll see that it's more ornamental than functional.
>
> Unfortunately, although Robineaux was a good accountant, he was also a rather vain and silly man. One day, Napoleon's Secretary of War made fun of Robineaux's sword. Words were exchanged, and a duel was held. Suffice it to say the outcome didn't work in Robineaux's favor, and Napoleon had to find a new treasurer.

Lester and I spoke a few months ago. He said that my telling others the same story I've just shared with you has resulted in over $75,000 worth of business for him. He said, "My reputation as the 'antiques with stories' guy has really separated me in a hugely competitive field." Stories are what gets you remembered. They're a powerful and important component of the overall branding strategy.

The third component of your personal brand is personality. There are many people who have created powerful brands around sheer personality such as Tony Robbins, Donald Trump and Dr. Phil. What these particular people have in common is that they are all very loud and very brash. As a result of that, they are very memorable. But this raises a question: do you have to be loud and outspoken to have a successful brand? Are the outsized personalities the only ones that can succeed? The answer is a resounding no.

Now, having said that, there is a certain advantage the showmen have that you or I don't. It is easier for them to gain recognition and become top of mind. However, that's a bit of a double-edged sword. Because they are so brash, they invite skepticism, and in many cases they appear a bit too slick, which obviously turns people off.

Based on periodic surveys we do of the very wealthy, these outsized personalities tend to play better with the middle class. If you are focused on attracting millionaires and billionaires as clients, you'll want a brand personality that is memorable but far more professional. The point is that you don't need to emulate the showmen. In fact, if you try to build a personal brand that doesn't reflect your authentic self, it will likely blow up in your face.

A case in point originates with a seminar that I attended many years ago. It was put on by T. Harv Eker, author of the very popular book *The Millionaire Mindset*. During the program's three days, I noticed that all of the presenters had a very similar style. In particular, they were very loud and very much in your face. They also made frequent use of the rhetorical question "Am I right or am I right?" to motivate the audience to buy whatever they were selling.

They'd start off presenting the price of their self-study programs as $10,000, but they added, "If you act now…I don't do this for everyone…my accountant would kill me if he knew I was doing this…you can have everything I'm offering today for just seven easy payments of $12.99!" We've all seen this pitch countless times on various info-commercials, but this was the first time I had actually seen anyone do it live and on stage. Given the lines that formed to buy the books and videos in the back of the room, I concluded that this style of selling must be pretty effective. It certainly wasn't anything that synced up with my own personal style, but I figured these people were selling a lot of stuff, so it must work.

I had the opportunity shortly thereafter to speak to an audience of business owners, so I thought I'd give this new approach a try. My presentation was laced with all the stock phrases I had learned. I'd say, "If you saw a $20 bill lying on the sidewalk, you'd pick it up. Am I right or am I right?" As I had learned at the seminar, I'd say anything to get people to say yes. I discounted my self-study program from $2,000 down to three easy payments of $49.95, and I sold precisely none of them.

Then I compounded my mistake by handing out evaluation forms to the audience. Over the years, I've spoken to tens of thousands of people, but one comment I got that day is seared into my memory bank. It simply said, "I loathed your presentation." The ultimate lesson I learned is that your brand personality needs to be authentic to you. That doesn't mean that you can't modify and enhance how you are perceived, but your personality must resonate truthfully with who you are as a person.

That said, if there is one mindset I'd try to adopt it would be enthusiastic positivity. The very rich are similar to everyone else in that they like enthusiasm. Sure, you can overdo it and come across as an over-eager lap dog, but barring that, enthusiasm is infectious. We like to be around people who are excited about what they are doing and who can't wait to share it with you.

The twin sibling of enthusiasm is positivity. We all like to associate with those who view the world with a glass-half-full perspective. When combined with exclusivity, enthusiasm and positivity can be used to create a powerful tool for selling to the wealthy. We can take a lesson from Amy McCarson, who sells fine art. She's been doing it for over twenty years, and the average price for a painting she sells is over $75,000. She says:

> When I started at the gallery, I noticed that all the other sales associates would welcome customers with a rather standard "Can I help you?" It's not a big shock that they would universally hear "Just browsing, thank you," and that would be the end of it. I also noticed that the associates were sort of snobby. It was almost as if they were above dealing with the public, which I thought was incredibly stupid.
>
> What I did was create a role that I played at work. It was my brand personality. To be honest, it wasn't terribly different from how I am in real life. I don't think it would have worked if it hadn't been. First, I wanted to send the message when you walked in the gallery that I was super excited you were there. It was wonderful that you took time out of your day

to visit with me. That, in and of itself, separated me from all the other associates, and it set the tone for how the customer and I interacted together.

My first question would be, "So what room in your house needs a bit of artistic refreshing?" This question almost always took people a bit by surprise, but it got them thinking. From there, the conversation would progress to the style of their house, what they liked in art, what they didn't, and what type of mood they were trying to create in the room. This last question was probably the most revealing, and it led to some very interesting conversations. Based on this I'd be able to direct the client to the paintings that were most appropriate for how they were trying to decorate that particular room. I'd connect the art to the mood they wanted. It was an extremely effective win-win sales technique.

Of course I'd still hear, "I'm just looking," but I don't give up so easily. I'd launch into one of my favorite stories about redecorating our bedroom and how my husband and I finally found the perfect painting because it represented both the love and the struggles we've endured over the years. Then I'd ask, "Would you like to see some of the works from this artist?" They almost always say that they would.

Now this next part is a bit sneaky, but since my personal brand is one of great positive enthusiasm, I can get away with it. I'd say, "Well, obviously I can't show you the exact painting since that's hanging above my bed at home, but here's what else he's done." Here's the thing about really rich people: they don't like to be told they can't have something. They'd look at the other paintings, but the seed had been planted that the really great piece of art, the one that would be perfect for them, wasn't available.

They'd look at the other works by the artist and, in the vast majority of cases, would ask, "You don't happen to have a picture of the one in your house, do you?" I'd whip out my phone and pull up the picture. You can guess what happens next. "Would you happen to be willing to sell that one?" I'd hem and haw and go on about how much the painting meant to my husband and me, but eventually I could be persuaded to sell it for what turned out to be a premium price.

And I wasn't being deceitful. My husband and I happen to like a lot of different art, and we really enjoy swapping out paintings in our house on a regular basis. So everything I told the client was the truth. Over the years, I've probably sold six dozen paintings that have hung in our house. In fact I've come to view our residence as an extension of the gallery.

But here's the secret sauce: it doesn't work unless your brand is one of positive enthusiasm. That's the way I am. At home, with my friends, and with my

> clients, what I've found is that people react positively to positive people. It really is the key to the success I've achieved.

Your personality is an often-overlooked but incredibly important component in your branding strategy. As long as the character you play is aligned with your authentic self, it is a positive amplification of your brand.

Your first opportunity to communicate your brand personality is on the landing page of your website. I think it is a huge mistake to not have a welcoming video. It doesn't have to be anything elaborate. For almost every business, a talking-head-style video is very effective. The message is simple:

- We're glad you are here.
- If you are a certain type of person or are seeking to solve a certain type of problem, you are in the right place.
- While I have your attention, let me give you a quick tour of the site.
- Please let me know if you have any questions or if I can be of further assistance.

This welcoming video provides you the chance to show your personality, and by doing so, you begin the all-important process of building a relationship. If you would like to see how this works, go to GentleRainMarketing.com and you can see the model in action.

Creating a personal business brand that will attract new affluent clients is important, but even more important is getting the word out about you and your services. That's what we're going to cover next.

Chapter 3:
Getting known

3.1 Client-acquisition metrics

In the rest of this book, we're going to focus on strategies for attracting affluent clients. Some of them will resonate with you, and others probably won't. That's fine. The key to effective marketing is to find something that works and that you enjoy doing. Most marketing fails not because the strategy was wrong, but rather because the individual simply gave up.

There are a couple of points to keep in mind. First, marketing, especially to the wealthy, takes time. You need to adopt the mindset that you're in this for the long haul. We all have a tendency to overestimate what we can achieve in a day and underestimate what we can achieve in a month.

Second, you'll be far more likely to stick with your plan if you enjoy the activity. For example, financial advisor Steve Rothingham enjoys making cold calls. He says:

> I think of it as a game. I've now been doing this for so long that I can pretty much anticipate what

> the person is going to say. There really aren't any objections I haven't heard before, so I view it as a sort of chess match. You say this, and I'll respond with that. Honestly, I think the fact that I'm having fun while I'm on the phone really helps with my success.

While cold calling works for Steve, it's not something that I would ever consider doing. I've always had a love for writing, though, and it's something I enjoy doing every day. Although I have done a lot of different things to get the word out about my services, writing has always been my go-to strategy.

Others enjoy speaking. Some hold events or make effective use of direct mail. I'll cover each of these methods and others as we move forward, but first we need to take a moment to discuss two important numbers that you need to pay attention to. These numbers can easily mean the difference between success and failure, and both are about cost. They will determine not only your profitability but also how you manage your client-acquisition strategy.

The first number is the price you pay for a lead. If you get your leads through advertising, it's pretty simple to determine: just divide the amount you spend on ads by the resulting number of leads. But suppose your leads come from networking, speeches, podcasting, events or social media? How do you track leads and determine cost in these cases? I'll explain how to track leads by sharing a brief story.

My personal business strategy for differentiating myself from the hundreds of other marketing consultants has been to write books. Over a twenty-year period, I wrote seven books, some of which were very successful. The challenge with this approach to lead generation is that, as with social media, speeches and networking, it is hard to determine precisely how much new business is generated by the activity. I had a general sense that my books helped grow my business, but if you're serious about your company, you need more than a general sense.

It wasn't until writing *The One Week Marketing Plan* that I figured out the solution to this problem. If you've read that book (and you should), you undoubtedly noticed that there was a coupon in the front offering a companion video series. All someone had to do was provide their name and email address on our website, and the video series would be sent to them automatically. Not surprisingly, a large percentage of the people who bought the book elected to opt in for the video series. I then had a way to track the number of leads I got from the book.

The video series is an example of what marketers call a *lead magnet*. Simply put, a lead magnet is something of value that you offer in exchange for a prospect raising their hand and identifying themselves as having an interest in your services. Lead magnets are often free reports, white papers or articles. The format really doesn't make much difference. The product just needs to be something that your prospects will have an interest in getting.

In all of your marketing, whether it be online, offline, on social media or wherever, you want to promote your free offer. This is how you will track the effectiveness of your marketing and determine how much a lead costs you. Social media is not free. It costs someone's time, and that needs to be accounted for. The same is true for speeches and networking. But tracking the cost of leads is just the first number. The second one is arguably more important.

How much does it cost you to get a new client? This second number determines how much you can spend on marketing. For example, if a typical client is worth $25,000 to you, a very conservative rule of thumb would be that you can spend $25,000. The idea is that any viable marketing plan will yield more than one client, so spending what you expect to make from one client means that you can expect to recover your costs. The more you can "go negative" before you need to make a profit, the more you can invest in marketing.

Remember that whoever can spend the most to attract a new client will win. That's a simple fact. If you can only spend $500 to get a new client and I can spend $25,000, I can be in a lot of places that you aren't. I can attract a lot more prospects, and all things being equal, I'll have a bigger business.

Here's another thing to keep in mind that's very important: if you don't know what your numbers are, human nature will make you nervous about spending any amount of money on marketing. When you don't see immediate results, you'll stop whatever you were doing or adopt a cost-cutting mindset. If you know your numbers, on the other hand, you'll have the confidence to continue, and knowledgeable perseverance is critical for success in attracting new affluent clients.

It's also more nuanced than that. There's an old marketing adage that says you should try a lot of stuff, see what works the best, and do more of that. It sounds trite, but it is very true. The challenge is that if you don't know your numbers, it's impossible to determine what is working and what is not.

Consider my experience. For about six months, I ran ads on Facebook. I got lots of leads, and my cost per lead was incredibly low. That sounds great, but there was a problem. Hardly any of the leads converted into paying clients. That is, although my cost per lead was extremely low, my cost per new client was extremely high. In fact, it was higher than any other marketing I was running at the time.

Not surprisingly, I cut the Facebook advertising and reallocated those dollars to what was working more cost effectively. I could only do that, however, because I knew what my cost per lead and cost per new client were. So, with those two numbers in mind, let's drill down on the various options for attracting affluent clients.

3.2 Your personal network

Given everything we've discussed so far, I hope we can all agree that when marketing to the affluent, the relationship needs to exist first and the sale will follow later. Certainly there are exceptions like impulse buys, but for the most part, the affluent do not work with those unfamiliar to them or their tribe.

Building a relationship from a cold start isn't easy. It requires energy, planning and patience. I'm a firm believer that any outfit that wants to do business with the ultra wealthy needs a multifaceted approach to bring in those clients. The proverbial low hanging fruit, though, is found in your existing network. Unfortunately, most of the clients I've worked with over the past thirty years hadn't done a particularly good job of growing and cultivating their network. Let's make sure that you do better.

There are three steps to building your network. The first is compiling a list of the people that constitute your network. You'll likely be surprised that the list is a lot larger than you thought. The second is to come up with some sort of excuse to get back in contact with those you've lost contact with. The third and final part is to develop a system to stay in regular contact with people so that you don't have to go through steps one and two again.

We'll start with step one and discuss how to compile your list. I like to use an exercise called "Who do I know and who might I know because" that I always use in a workshop called *Marketing to the Affluent*. In order for the exercise to work, you need to approach it as a data dump rather than trying to develop a curated list. Slicing and dicing to determine who should really be an active part of your network will come later.

You can start the exercise by asking yourself, "Who do I know because I went to high school?" Remember that at this stage I don't want you to filter the names that you come up with. Your list will include close friends, people you played sports with, people who co-starred in the school play, people you carpooled with, and so on. Write down everyone that comes to mind, and don't forget about those who were a class or two ahead of or behind you.

The first people you want to put on the list are those you knew personally no matter how casually, but that's just the beginning. Google your high school and see what notable people have graduated from there. This is a group of people that you *might* know because you went to a certain school. Such people are connections, too, and you may be surprised by how things pan out if you contact them.

For example, I went to the Boston area prep school Buckingham Browne & Nichols, and the alumni association does a marvelous job updating everyone about what alumni are doing. Celebrity hotelier Andre Balazs of Chateau Marmount, Chilten Firehouse, and The Standard was a couple of years behind me. I can't claim that we even knew each other casually when we were at prep school, yet that alumni connection was enough to start a relationship that resulted in him introducing me to people who later became clients.

You'll want to repeat this same drill for any colleges or graduate schools you've attended and for the various companies that you have worked for. Connections from my days at PepsiCo and Kraft Foods have been invaluable over the years. Again, remember that we are just compiling the list. Don't filter it, and don't make the mistake of saying, "Well, s/he wouldn't remember me." In fact, let's work on the assumption that they won't remember you. Later, I'll share with you an easy method for reconnecting that takes just a few minutes.

To continue adding to the list, ask yourself, "Who do I know because I read books?" This is one of my personal favorites. Perhaps it's because I've written eight books (including the highly recommended *One Week Marketing Plan*) or because I appreciate the lonely nature of being a writer. When you combine this solitary pursuit with the desire for appreciation that all authors have, it becomes surprisingly easy to develop relationships.

My own experience again offers a case in point. Since I specialize in marketing to the affluent, I'm a voracious reader of books that focus on the rich. Many years ago, I sent a note to Dominick Dunne, who wrote many bestsellers about the peccadilloes of the wealthy. It started out "I don't normally write letters like this…" I know that sounds a bit like how letters to Penthouse Forum tend to start, but it's a surprisingly effective way to get attention. I wasn't really expecting to hear back, but somewhat to my surprise, I did. Over the next ten years, Dominick offered helpful insights on the tribal nature of the rich. I remain extremely grateful that he shared his perspective.

In a related example, I had the opportunity a few years back to work with some clients in Singapore and South Asia. Although I had a hunch that marketing to the affluent would be different in these cultures, I wasn't entirely sure how. I had enjoyed Kevin Kwan's *Crazy Rich Asians* saga, so I decided to reach out to him.

As in the previous case, I didn't expect much, but I was pleasantly surprised when he emailed back. Kevin was extremely generous and provided a wonderful perspective on the unique cultural customs of the wealthy in Asia. Suffice it to say if you're a reader (and you really should be), connecting with authors can both enrich your knowledge base and provide introductions that might otherwise be extremely difficult to get.

As we continue to compile our list of connections, we ought to be wary of the fallacy of social media. Unfortunately, in this day and age, we tend to think of "connections" as people with whom we have a social media relationship. That's extremely limiting, and to be honest, most of your Facebook or Instagram connections aren't worth much. Certainly there are exceptions, but most of the online connections that will ever amount to anything are on LinkedIn. Focus your efforts there.

Who else do you know? The list is really only limited by your imagination. Who do you know because you live in the neighborhood you live in? Who do you know because of the clubs you belong to, because of the sports you play, or because of your other hobbies and activities? Who do you know because you have children? Think about what you engage in, where you socialize, and what occurs on a day-to-day basis. Who do you know as a result of those things?

It's extremely important to recognize that this exercise will only work if you write the names down. Simply thinking about who might be in your network isn't enough. Write the names down and don't filter. As I said, at this stage, it's just a data dump. One participant in our class said that he almost didn't write down the name of his kids' babysitter. His initial thought was "Who could she possibly know?" Then he remembered who else she babysat for.

Let's now turn our attention to how to connect with the people on your list. As a start, I'd go through the list and sort the names into three groups: prospects you know personally, prospects you know casually, and people who could connect you to prospects. As you do this, ask yourself, "What might be an excuse or reason to connect or reconnect with this person?" If nothing comes to mind, don't worry. I'll give you a few ideas shortly.

Remember that the first goal is to create and develop a relationship. As much as you might wish that it could be otherwise, you are not yet ready to pitch your services. The affluent will not buy from you unless you have a relationship with them or with someone they trust.

Without further ado, let's reach out to the people on your list. If you're contacting someone you actually know, you could send an email with a personal variation of the following:

> I've been terribly remiss in not doing a better job of staying in touch with people who meant a lot to me at school / when we worked together / however you know them. I thought I would reach out to see how you are doing.

Next, give a brief update on what you have been doing. Make sure that it does not sound the least bit "salesy." Conclude with a call to action like "I was hoping that you might have fifteen minutes free over the next couple of weeks for me to pick your brain about (a topic)." A message like this has a good chance of progressing your relationship with its recipient.

You can modify your messaging a bit to reach out to someone with whom you have only a casual relationship. As readers of mine know, I'm a firm believer in the importance of writing a blog and, ultimately, books. It's with the casual acquaintance that this proves invaluable. For example, I might swap out the call to action above with something like:

> I'm working on an article (or book) about (topic). I could really use your perspective on (something very specific that I know this person would have knowledge about). Your expertise and insight would be enormously helpful. Do you have twenty minutes available sometime over the next two weeks for a quick chat?

Everyone wants to feel important, and one of the easiest ways to get people to connect with you is to play to that fundamental human need. If the writing pretext isn't appropriate for you, come up with another way that you might derive some genuine value from their input.

When it comes to connecting with people who might be able to refer you to a prospect, we recommend something different. Over the years, we've tried all sorts of different approaches on behalf of our clients. Nothing has generated a better response than brutal honesty. Simply craft a message stating the following:

- This is who I am
- This is what I'd like
- This is the benefit of referring me

- Can you help?
- Sincere thanks

Once you've reached out to your connections, you'll need to systematically follow up. It would be great if all of your outreach would be acted upon, but the reality is that you'll get a deafening silence from far more people than you would hope. We suggest following the "rule of three." Simply put, make three sincere attempts to reach a person. Vary the initial message slightly each time, but be consistent with the call to action. If you don't hear anything back after three attempts, my personal recommendation is to move on to other prospects.

Having said that, it's worth mentioning the experience of an associate of mine who very much wanted to connect with Richard Branson. It took eighty-three messages, but the sheer persistence ultimately won the day. Perhaps that might be worthwhile for your personal dream connection, but realistically, most of us don't have the patience or temperament to make that level of concerted effort.

Once you've established or reestablished a relationship, you'll need a strategy for staying in touch. If you use the article-writing pretext, you'll certainly want to send them a copy of the piece once it's done. Beyond that, it's a matter of how often you think you need to be in contact in order to maintain their awareness about you. My personal advice would be to stay in touch at least once per month. You can certainly do it more frequently as long as you are communicating something of value and interest.

My personal philosophy is to send everyone an update on any

new content that you produce. For me and many of my clients, this means announcing a new blog article every week. We have found that people don't mind a weekly communication, but more than once per week tends to be too much. There are many automated systems that you can use to disseminate your messages, and choosing one is more a matter of personal preference than anything else.

One final word about ongoing communication: write like you speak. Your communication should have a conversational tone to it. Remember, everything we are doing at this stage is to build a relationship. This is also why I also suggest using video as a means of staying in touch if you're comfortable with it.

For years I've used the old Walt Disney approach to the content I send out. Back in the day, Walt would appear at the very beginning of every show to tell you what that evening's feature was about. By doing this, he became a person that people felt they knew, even if they never actually met him. You should strive for the same thing.

Next, let's take a moment to discuss referrals, which provide a powerful supplement to your networking efforts. Referrals come from two primary sources: people who are similar to your prospective clients and the trusted advisors of those prospects. You want to cultivate relationships with both groups.

You can start by seeking referrals from your existing clients, and you can improve the quality of the referrals you get by using the power of exclusivity. To do this, meet personally with your top clients. Specifically, meet with the type of client that you'd like to have more of. Tell them that you've just finished your annual business plan, and say that you've determined that you can add a limited number of new clients *like them* to your practice. Say, "Before I add them in the traditional way, is there anyone that you would like to recommend?" Then stop talking and wait.

Assuming you're doing great work for the client, this will work in large part because you are positioning it as a very limited offer. Having only a few spots available leverages the power of scarcity. The person you are speaking with will naturally assume that you are talking with your other top clients and that, as a result, the spots will fill quickly.

You are layering the psychological power of urgency on top of exclusivity, which is a very effective technique. Ultimately, exclusivity should be a critical part of your branding position. Everything you do should convey the message that your services are for an extremely targeted and limited niche. You want to use exclusivity as a tool for attracting affluent clients to your business.

Let's now discuss expanding your network by building relationships with the trusted advisors of the rich. When we hear the term "trusted advisor," we tend to only think of accountants, financial planners and lawyers. I want you to think about the term more generally. In fact, most of the people that provide services to high-net-worth individuals are trusted advisors.

In many cases, a relationship develops over time that might be best described as a paid friend. Research by Huron Wealth supports the conclusion that the wealthy have few traditional friends due to reasons that are easy to guess. Paid friends meet the need for human connection that is important to everyone. As in any friendship, paid or not, conversations cover a wide variety of topics. This presents an interesting relationship-building opportunity if it is handled in the right way.

For example, one of our clients runs a very high-end, bespoke travel club. Participation in the club requires a six-figure enrollment fee. Although his traditional marketing methods provided excellent results, he realized that there was a large, untapped market waiting to be cultivated.

This realization came about when he surveyed his clients about how they had initially heard about him. (Note that if you are not doing this on a regular basis, you really should be.) About two thirds of them had heard about him from his appearances in the media, from his books, or from his advertisements in luxury publications. However, the other third had heard about him from other people who provide services to the wealthy. In his particular case, it was hairdressers.

"Think about it," he recounted to me. "You're in the chair getting your hair done, and what do you do? You chat. And what do you talk about? Well, among the wealthy, travel is a huge activity." This insight led to a very specific marketing plan. He reached out to high-end hair stylists in five target cities. A referral program was established, and select stylists were offered free vacations.

This was similar in some ways to the time-honored practice of Las Vegas casinos offering free show tickets to cab and limo drivers. You want to think about who might be in a position to inform others about your services, and you want to develop a plan to reach out to that specific audience. In the case of the stylists, the results were significant. Referrals from just this one source tripled in less than twelve months.

I want you to think about who the wealthy have service relationships with. A partial list could include insurance agents, financial advisors, real estate agents, luxury retailers, art gallery owners, interior designers, personal trainers, chiropractors, yoga instructors, and hairdressers. The full list could include almost anyone with whom a prospect might spend one-on-one time. One way to construct this list is to ask your existing wealthy clients who they work with for various types of services.

When building relationships with the advisors to the wealthy, you want to think about what their wants and needs are and what you could do to help them. Go beyond the immediate and obvious realization that they probably want more clients. Sometimes that's not even the case. Focus instead on their hobbies, activities, and other things that they're interested in.

Once you've identified what those things are, remember that for every interest there is an influencer. An influencer is someone who has built a reputation for expertise or for knowledge of trends in their field. They might be the author of a book, or they might have a large social media presence. Research a topic on Amazon or on YouTube to identify the well known people in that field. These are the people that the advisors to the wealthy would be interested in hearing from. Can you arrange an event where an influencer or expert would speak? Can you connect an advisor with an influencer directly?

I never would have guessed this, but many yoga instructors in South Carolina have a strong interest in Shag Dancing. Do you want to build relationships with these people? Sponsor a private Shag event. This is how one art dealer developed a relationship with a yoga instructor who had a lot of very wealthy clients. She estimated to me that this one event eventually resulted in $750,000 in sales for her gallery.

Obviously, what we are doing here is playing the long game. Your competition is banging away directly at the wealthy prospects and hoping to get their attention. They don't really have anything original to say. They usually try some variation of "I thought it would be good for us to connect" or, even worse, "I have a solution/process/fintech thing that's truly unique." We can do a lot better than that.

Chapter 4:
Trojan Horse marketing

4.1 Leveraging their interests

There is certainly no shortage of ways to attract new clients, so where do we start? How do we decide on the best marketing strategy for your business? We can sort the various options into three general categories: push marketing, pull marketing and Trojan Horse marketing.

As the name implies, push marketing strategies involve pushing your expertise out to a specific community. Direct mail, print and online advertising, and cold calling are all examples of push marketing. The most effective push marketing strategy involves offering a lead magnet such as a free report or video and hoping for a reasonable response rate.

If you select your audience correctly, push marketing can work very well, but that's a big if. The obvious risk is that you don't know whether anyone is interested in the services you offer. A marketing campaign to one audience can yield big returns while the exact same campaign presented to a slightly different audience yields nothing.

Pull marketing is a different beast. As the name would imply, this form of marketing involves attracting people who are actively seeking solutions to a particular problem. Pull marketing includes search engine optimization (SEO) and all forms of advertising. I'll talk in depth about pull marketing strategies later, but for now I want to focus on the third type: Trojan Horse marketing.

This approach is more stealthy. Simply put, it's about leveraging hobbies, interests and educational opportunities to get in with the rich. Let's start with an example involving hobbies and interests. Luxury realtor Jon Grauman of The Agency employs a clever marketing technique: he shoots periodic videos in which he and a client share a bottle of wine.

As Jon says, "I try to pair the wine with the personality of the person I'm speaking with." What makes this approach particularly effective is that Jon is tapping into what he knows is an interest of his highly affluent target audience. It is a lesson that virtually any business can adopt as a part of their marketing plan.

In order for this strategy to work, it needs to involve an interest that's shared by a lot of rich people, and the interest needs to be something that you're either interested in or could realistically become interested in. I have a passion for Silver Age Marvel comic books, but while this topic attracts some affluent aficionados, it tends to be more of interest to the middle class. So, what are the rich interested in?

The interests of the very wealthy tend to cluster around certain topics. The big ones are: wine, travel, watches, fashion, spirituality, and certain sports, but mostly golf. If your natural hobbies and interests trend more to popular culture, the question then becomes what interests *could* you develop.

As we go through the list, take note of what resonates with you. This is important since if you have absolutely no interest in, let's say, wine, it will be hard to put together a sustained marketing effort around it. Remember that the failure of any marketing initiative has more to do with simply giving up than anything else.

Whatever topic you choose, you need to be able to talk about it. Simply showing up at a Ferrari enthusiast's event when you know nothing about the cars is going to be a waste of time. The whole premise behind this marketing strategy is to build relationships, and in order to do that, you need to be able to talk knowledgeably and engagingly about your topic. Alex Robertson, a Dallas-based interior designer, has the following to say on the matter:

> I didn't think my interest in collecting vintage lunch boxes would lend itself to meeting a lot of affluent clients. However, I had a stamp collection when I was a kid, and although I dropped the hobby later in life, I'd always had a mild interest in it. That said, I really didn't have a lot of knowledge about the current stamp collecting scene.
>
> The great news is that you can learn pretty much anything online if you're willing to invest the time. I knew the stamp collecting community here in Dallas is pretty robust, so I made a plan to learn all I could for

> six months before I attended my first meeting. I found that you didn't need to be an expert on everything, but rather become really knowledgeable about a niche area. My focus was on first-day covers, which enabled me to strike up conversations with a number of wealthy enthusiasts. Over time, being a member of this group produced two new clients.

Keep in mind that networking at these events is a two-way street. Alice Cheng, founder and CEO of the hospitality networking and job-matching site Culinary Agents, advises, "During the conversation, actually listen, and think about how you can help the person you're talking with. People will be more likely to help you if they think you can help them." With that in mind, let's explore more deeply the potential areas of interest that you might want to focus on. We'll begin with wine.

From national tastings such as Wine Spectator's Top 100 to local meetups and regional events, there is no shortage of wine-related activity. Since such events tend to be very well attended, it's a good idea to set a specific goal for a meeting. Whenever possible, do your research about who will be attending, and select three people that you want to meet. Luxury retailer Holly Gresham concurs and says, "I always find that I get far better results when I go to a meeting with a specific plan rather than a general objective of just meeting people."

Unlike the throngs of wine connoisseurs, the watch community is surprisingly tight knit, although it still offers a variety of ways to learn and to connect with fellow enthusiasts. Some of the best resources for learning about watch collecting and for staying current are blogs like *Watchnonista* and *Hodinkee*. Mainstream publications including *Robb Report* and *Forbes* also have staff dedicated to the watch industry.

One group that is definitely worth checking out is RedBar, a large international network of collectors that meets regularly to discuss watch collecting. Although watch collectors tend to be quite wealthy, what sets RedBar apart is the unpretentious and easygoing vibe of the group. As Sophie Rindler of RedBar's Miami chapter says, "In order to preserve the culture of the group, we try to welcome fellow watch enthusiasts who are cool, nice to others, and not a snob."

Moving on from watches, if there is one sporting interest that is common among wealthy individuals, it's golf. Since the game is typically played in groups of four, it lends itself to networking. Insurance broker Tom Adamson once worked with a junior team member who struggled to build relationships with the wealthy. As he describes it:

> He just wasn't making any headway at networking events and was really struggling since he's pretty introverted. By chance, I learned that he was actually a pretty accomplished golfer, although he only played with his buddies on the weekend.
>
> What was completely obvious to me never occurred to him. We signed him up for probably a dozen

> charity golf events. Rich guys love playing with a really good golfer, so this was a true no-brainer. Suffice it to say it completely turned his book of business around. I guess because he was so used to playing golf as purely a social activity, he never thought about the business development potential.

While both men and women play golf, it tends to be more popular with men. Do you want to connect with affluent women? Spirituality is an overlooked area of interest. Insurance broker Eric St. James tells us:

> We had some female clients but wanted more. Based on a survey, we determined that there was a deep interest in spirituality among women in our target markets. At our firm, we have team members focus on specific demographics or clusters of potential clients. One member also had an interest in spirituality and yoga, and we encouraged her to get involved in the community. She started an after-hours group called Pints & Poses that was held at a local brew pub. I'll admit I was a bit skeptical, but it turned out to be a great success.

It's worth thinking about these areas of interest not only in terms of meetings you might attend, but also in terms of events you might host yourself. Often referred to as an "intimate client event," a small gathering that focuses on something of interest to your particular niche audience can be a fantastic tool. It's important to remember that intimate client events do not focus at all on your solution, your business, or what you want your prospect to buy from you. They are all about relationship building.

I've worked with clients who put together intimate client events around stamps, art, golf, boating and coins. One of my favorites, and one in which I was a participant, focused on trap shooting. This was an extremely well executed event that served two purposes for the sponsor. It both cemented relationships with existing clients and provided an opportunity to meet prospective clients.

My friend Carl invited me to the event. His financial advisor hosted it, and to be perfectly honest, I initially had zero interest. I really didn't want to meet "yet another financial advisor with some sort of unique financial strategy," and I didn't really have any understanding of what trap shooting was all about. Carl sent me the invitation anyway, and I'll admit it was a classy invitation.

The letter that accompanied the formal invitation said that this was purely a social event. It emphasized that there would be no pitching or discussion of business. What really got my attention was that the host described the event as "gold with guns." Now, I live in the South, and I'm a guy. The appeal to go shoot at stuff was pretty strong.

There were twelve of us in attendance. The advisor who sponsored the event was true to his word, and there was absolutely no pitching or discussion of his business. That was extremely important, because if intimate client events are going to work, people have to feel comfortable bringing their friends along.

A professional photographer was on hand to take pictures of us attempting not to shoot each other, and this provided a great excuse for the host to get back in touch. The photographs brought the law of reciprocity into play, so I was happy to accept his invitation for lunch. As you might expect, lunch included a more business-focused conversation. The net result of the event was that the advisor obtained two new clients with over $10 million to invest.

Trojan Horse marketing requires thinking about ways to be less obvious with your client-attraction efforts. For example, I once encountered a twist on the traditional educational seminar. Usually, the idea of attracting clients in this way evokes an image of the free investment, insurance or real estate seminar. Unfortunately, these events rarely attract the type of client the sponsor really wants. So, what type of education works?

For a client who leased airplanes to ultra-high-net-worth individuals, we began by identifying the types of hobbies their clients engage in. This was achieved through a short survey of their existing clients, which had the additional benefit of being a wonderful way to reconnect. After reviewing the survey results, it was apparent that art collecting was at the top of the list.

Rather than simply hire an art expert to conduct a one-time lecture, we decided to develop an educational series around the topic. Sessions included:

1. Fundamentals of developing an art collection and trusted resources to advise you
2. Appreciation and what categories are likely to appreciate the most in the next ten to fifteen years
3. Trends in art collection: arbitrage and fractional ownership
4. Tax and hidden financial implications of art collection

Additionally, rather than offer the series for free, we charged a nominal fee to enroll. Naturally, we assembled a prestigious group of presenters, the event was held in an appropriate venue, and the overall experience was first class. Yes, this required a considerable amount of work and planning, but it was well worth the investment.

Flash forward six months, and it turns out that the lecture series produced $15 million in new revenue. What's more, client relationships in the private aviation field often last for decades, so the total return from this marketing effort will likely be considerably higher. Think about identifying the hobbies that your clients engage in, and develop an educational program around that.

Aside from an educational series focused on hobbies, what else might you consider? You could give some thought to the children of the affluent. They tend to be clustered at a small number of private day and boarding schools. For one campaign, we decided to focus on a particular prestigious private boarding school. The school is well known for educating the children of European royalty, billionaires and celebrities.

As one might imagine, some of these children have appallingly poor social skills. This is recognized both by the school's administrators and by a high percentage of their parents. Over the course of six months, we worked with the staff of the school to create a class that was referred to by the students as Charm School. Despite the somewhat snarky title, it was hugely popular.

While not guaranteeing that anyone would do business with our client, the establishment of the course enabled them to connect with the students' parents in a variety of ways. Most notable among the program's outreach methods was an event held on campus that allowed our client, the students' parents and the students to interact. This event was a creative way to establish an initial connection with prospective clients that were otherwise very elusive. The hard work and investment of time paid off with seven new clients for the sponsor.

Trojan Horse marketing can be extremely effective for attracting new clients, especially when it is coupled with the other two forms of marketing. Let's take a look at pull marketing next.

Chapter 5:
Pull marketing

As you'll recall, pull marketing is about figuratively pulling your prospective affluent clients toward you. There are a variety of options including writing blogs and books, speaking in public, sharing on social media, and performing traditional advertising. We'll discuss each of these methods in the pages to come, but first we'll set the tone by mentioning some overarching themes to keep in mind.

One theme that works particularly well with the wealthy is FOMO, the fear of missing out. There is a basic human desire to want the things that we can't have, and like most other people, the rich imagine that there might be something great out there just around the corner. They feel like whatever it is might be really cool if only they could find it.

How do we leverage this in our marketing to the affluent? In one word: exclusivity. Scarcity and exclusivity have long been recognized as powerful psychological tools. They are used to make prospects believe that they'll miss out on an interesting product or service. I'm often surprised that more businesses that target the ultra-rich don't use this as a core marketing theme. For example, *Financial Times* noted recently that "Rich people take part in television reality shows despite the obvious downsides because it gives them something they don't have: fame." The more your products or services are available to everyone, the less desirable you will be to the wealthy tribe you most want to do business with.

So, how specifically can you use FOMO and related ideas to attract wealthy clients? There are several options to consider. The first is limiting availability. Communicate to the prospect that due to the nature of your bespoke services, you are only able to work with a small number of clients at a time. You can expand on this idea by using waiting lists. As Lisa Furze points out in her marvelous book *The Velvet Rope Strategy*, it's the line of people waiting to get into the club that makes it seem all the more desirable. One of our clients, a concierge physician, saw signups for her practice quadruple when she put a waiting list in place.

Qualifying is another tool at your disposal. The goal of any affluent marketing campaign is to actually speak with the prospective client. However, it is important that you communicate that you "can't help everyone." Shift the balance so that prospects are convincing you that they are a good fit for your business. You can accomplish this by initially communicating the benefits people get from speaking with you and then equally explicitly communicating who you work with and who you don't.

You might also make judicious use of deadlines. A client who owns a prestigious art gallery might offer only a limited, eighteen-hour window in which people can sign up for a preview exhibition. Once the deadline has passed, he will hold firm and "regretfully" inform inquirers that the enrollment period has ended. By doing so, he will train his potential clients to take his deadlines seriously, and this will increase the desire to attend.

Finally, consider making exclusive invitations. Many of our clients have had great success hosting small, intimate gatherings focused on topics of interest to the wealthy. The typical wealth-planning seminar has been done to death and won't attract the ultra-wealthy, but a lecture by an expert in art, coins, watches or other interests of the affluent is likely to break through the clutter of invitations.

Now that you have a general sense for what kind of messaging to use, let's get more specific about what to do.

5.1 Books

Should you write a book? The answer isn't a simple yes or no. Obviously, writing a book is a big undertaking, so the question for you is actually "Is it worth doing?" I've written eight books over the past thirty years. *Unique Sales Stories* and *The One Week Marketing Plan* were very successful, two never gained much traction, and the rest sort of fell in between. All in all, writing books has been my single best tool for attracting new clients and growing my business.

There are some important things to keep in mind, however. Most books never get published because enthusiasm dissipates. As Mark Twain said, "It's easy to get enthusiastic about something. The real skill is staying enthusiastic." That's especially true when it comes to writing a book, so my first piece of advice is to make sure that you're really committed to the project. You have to embrace the value and importance of publishing your book. It can't be something that would be nice to do, but rather you need to think of it as fundamental to your overall business brand.

Putting all that aside, there is a particular benefit to writing a book for anyone who desires to attract affluent clients. Remember, the very rich will tend to do business with one of three types of people:

1. Those they personally know or those that travel in their social circles
2. Those that are referred to them by those in the first group
3. Those who are recognized experts in their field

Even though our society has evolved from one of readers to one of viewers, books still play an outsized role in establishing people as recognized experts in their field. Blogs, videos, articles, and speaking are valuable for positioning yourself, but nothing is as powerful as a book.

My personal approach is to extensively outline the book and to work with an editor during the writing process. Since I produce a weekly blog, the material I write is immediately uploaded to the book document. Although I don't make it a point of saying in my blog that "This will be Chapter 7 of my forthcoming book," one could read my books' content in advance just by being a subscriber of mine. I've found that this doesn't hurt sales once the book comes out, and serializing a book in this manner is actually a time-honored tradition that dates back to Charles Dickens.

I've spoken with other authors, and most of them have a particular time of day at which it's easiest for them to write. I usually find that I'm at my most creative an hour or so after I get up and then once again in the early afternoon. I try to write something every day. It doesn't have to be good, and I wind up trashing the previous day's effort regularly. However, I firmly believe that you need to try to put your fingers on the keyboard every day.

There are a lot of excellent programs that teach both writing technique and motivation. My personal favorites are the classes produced by American Writers & Artists found at AWAI.com. Although they focus on copywriting, the skills they teach can benefit any nonfiction writer. Their material is definitely worth checking out.

Do you want a shortcut for writing a book that takes all the pain out of the process? Of course you do. I'll tell you the absolute easiest way to write a book. The key is to remember that people buy a solution. They want to move from where they currently are to a point at which they have achieved very specific goals. Ideally, they'll do this with your help.

The first simple task is to write out the steps that the reader needs to take in order to achieve the success he or she wants. There are usually between eight and ten milestones that they would need to reach. Once that's done, outline for each milestone the critical actions that need to be taken. Think about the questions your clients typically ask and about the problems or issues they face. Write all of those down as a series of bullet points.

I'll guess that you've had to make a number of PowerPoint presentations in your life. Most of us have. I next want you to literally create a PowerPoint presentation based on the outline you've created. Once that's done, perform the presentation to a friend or an empty room and record it. You could practice it a couple of times first if you want to, but don't worry about perfecting it, because nobody who might care how it sounds is going to hear it.

Once you have the recording, send it to Rev.com and get them to transcribe it. It will cost you $1.50 per minute, so this will probably cost you less than $200. It's critical that when you get the transcription back you do not read it. If you do, you'll just get depressed. None of us sound particularly great at this stage in the book development process.

Once you have the transcription file, go to Fiverr.com and search for someone who proofreads, edits and cleans up transcriptions. There are a lot of people who do that sort of work, so just select the one with the highest rating. Again, this isn't going to cost a lot of money. When you get the edited file back, go ahead and read through it. You'll probably want to make some changes, but the heavy lifting has been done, and you now have most of your book written.

Next, go to Upwork.com and find someone who will do the layout work and create a cover for your book. When I republished my book *Unique Sales Stories*, I paid $300 for these services. The person who does this work will usually also have the ability to upload the files to Amazon so that you can use their Kindle Direct Publishing program. KDP will make your book available on Amazon as both a paperback and a Kindle ebook.

That's all there is to it. You're now a published author. It couldn't be easier. Now that you know at least one way that will definitely work, you should be more confident and comfortable thinking through the process. That being the case, let's shift our focus to two critical areas that you need to think about early on in the writing process: who is going to publish your book, and publicity and advertising.

Options for publishing your book include self-publishing and using a traditional publisher. I've done both, and there are some tradeoffs. Traditional publishers give an author a level of credibility that self-publishing doesn't. This is largely due to the hoops one has to jump through in order to get accepted by a traditional publisher. You need to submit a proposal, and you usually need to be represented by an agent. The review process can be long and in depth. All of this means that books published by a traditional publisher have been highly vetted.

Obviously, there's no vetting that takes place in self-publishing aside from the efforts of the author. I'm not suggesting that you shouldn't self-publish, but if you do, make the effort to have your book look as professional as possible. That means hiring a cover designer and a really good copy editor. I'd also suggest creating a publishing company name so that your book doesn't scream "I'm doing this on Amazon." (That said, Amazon's KDP publishing program stands heads and shoulders above other self publishing options.)

Remember, the reason you're writing the book in the first place is to build credibility, so having it look professional is crucial. I cannot emphasize enough how important your cover is. Don't try to do it yourself. Hire someone. You can find cover designers by searching on the internet or on the freelancing site Upwork. Your cover will inspire people to either pause to learn more about your book or to quickly pass it by. You can recommend designs from other books that you find attractive, but leave the actual design to someone who has done this many times before.

It came as a bit of a surprise to me that when creating your cover, you are better off mimicking (but not outright copying) the look of other books in your genre. Doing so will dramatically increase your sales. This is one of the reasons why romance novels all tend to follow an established formula. The same is true for business books. Identify popular books in your genre and use their style as a jumping off point in the discussion with your designer.

I have one other important point about writing your book: most people focus on the benefits that will come once the book is published, but that's a bit short sighted. In fact, the writing process itself can be a very powerful client-attraction tool. It all hinges on the concept of McGuffins.

The term "McMuffin" originally referred to a plot device in a fiction novel, but in our case, it refers to the collection of reasons or excuses you create to initiate contact and stay in touch with prospective clients. Writing a book offers you very powerful and easy-to-implement excuses to reach out to people who might otherwise never return your calls. The book-writing McGuffins are really powerful, in part because of ego: most people rather like the idea of being quoted in a book.

To give your request an air of legitimacy, I suggest you position your request for an interview by saying, "I have a contract with McGraw Hill (or whatever publisher you're contracted with), and I was hoping to feature you in my forthcoming book (*Really Catchy Title*)." What if you don't have a publisher yet or are self-publishing? That's no problem. Simply create a publishing house name of your own.

You'll be amazed at who you can get to participate in your book project. I'd encourage you to think not only of people who would be potential clients but also of those who might be willing to promote your book once it comes out. When I was starting to write *The One Week Marketing Plan,* I compiled two lists. The first contained the names of people I wanted to interview who might become clients. The second contained names of people featured in the book who might want to promote the book to their audience. To make a long story short, over fifty people participated in my project, and this strategy led to the book becoming a bestseller and to me establishing more than two dozen new client relationships.

Interviewing people for book content is great, but don't overlook the McGuffin of getting people to write promotional blurbs for the book. It's a wonderful excuse to reach out to people. You offer to send them an advance copy of your book, and then a couple of weeks later, you follow up to see if they would be willing to write a short promotional review. Truth be told, you can't be sure how many people actually read the book, but the fact that you send them an advance copy leverages the power of reciprocity in your favor.

I hear all the time that people would be more than happy to provide a review, but they'd prefer that I write it. Talk about a win-win situation. Any time you write a testimonial, think about the points of resistance people have about the service you offer. Focus your testimonials in a way that preempts any reason that someone might not do business with you. For example, here is the review quote I wrote for Robert Bloom, former CEO of advertising giant Publicis:

> Many business owners worry that implementing a marketing system will be too difficult, too complicated, and too expensive. What's great about Mark Satterfield's *The One Week Marketing Plan* is that it's practical and easy to implement, and it doesn't cost you an arm and a leg. Every business owner needs to read this.

For Peter Vantine, a member of the marketing faculty at Georgia Tech's College of Business, I wrote, "If your company is seeking a better ROI on its marketing investment, you'll find Mark Satterfield's *The One Week Marketing Plan* to be definitely worth reading. His approach is efficient, measurable, and simple to execute." As you can see with these two quotes, I'm addressing very real and common concerns that many businesses have about marketing. Rather than me trying to overcome these objections, it's far more effective to have others fight that battle.

Promotions are another important thing you'll need to think about and budget for before taking on this project. Since it is so easy to self-publish, the sheer number of books being produced each year has increased dramatically. You'll need to have a plan in place to get the word out. Speaking from personal experience, I can tell you that the two bestsellers I wrote didn't become bestsellers just because they were better books. They sold a lot of copies because I put considerable time and effort into promoting them.

As a result of partnering with some great PR advisors, one of my books was featured both in the national press and in highly focused business publications. An interview on ESPN radio ultimately resulted in a $250,000 client. For that interview, we referred to my book on telling stories while discussing stories told by famous Super Bowl ads. The campaign took a lot of effort, but the results were great.

The number of books I sell isn't the most important metric to me. I am most interested in how much new business my company gets as a result of the books. In my most recent book, *The One Week Marketing Plan*, I offered a coupon for a free companion video series that people could get by going to a specific website. That enabled me to track the direct, tangible results, and it was a highly effective way to continue building relationships with those who bought the book. There is a similar offer in the front of this book that I hope you'll take advantage of. You can also find it by visiting our website www.GentleRainMarketing.com.

To finish our discussion of your book, let's discuss the role of advertising. There are several options to consider. First, advertising in places that your prospective clients read can be highly effective for promoting your book. Ads in *The Robb Report*, *Financial Times*, or specialty trade publications can work, as can banner ads on websites. However, ads are expensive.

Luckily, there are ways to increase the ROI on an ad. First and foremost, make sure the ad is laid out by a professional. It needs to catch the eye, intrigue the mind, and motivate the viewer to want to click on it. This is the domain of a graphic artist or ad layout designer, so don't do this yourself.

As long as space permits, there's nothing wrong with mentioning that the book is available on Amazon and where other fine books are sold, but my personal recommendation is to have the prospect visit your website to read one chapter for free. This free chapter doesn't necessarily need to be the first one in the book.

I would select the chapter that you think has the most curiosity value for your target audience. For example, when marketing his *4 Hour Body* book, Tim Ferris used this approach by heavily hyping the chapter on the 15 Minute Orgasm. Most of us don't have something quite so sensational to announce, but there is usually one chapter in your book that stands out from the others.

The benefit of having your ad's call to action direct people to your website is that it enables you to build your list. When people arrive at your website or at a webpage set up specifically for the book promotion, they should be presented with a short opt-in form. They will enter their name and email address so that the system can send them the free chapter via email. Although your list of followers and connections on social media is important, your personal list of subscribers is the most valuable. From a broader business perspective, you always want to be focused on growing the length of your subscriber list.

Another mode of advertising that is worth considering is Amazon Marketing Services. This program puts your ad in front of book buyers when they search for books by topic or by title. Publisher Rocket is a helpful and informative resource on Amazon Marketing Services, and I'd recommend looking them up for more information.

In summary, if you're focused on the affluent market, there is no other single weapon in your arsenal that is as powerful as writing a book. This is not to say that you can't be successful without a book, but if you're serious about becoming one of the highly recognized experts in your field, it's definitely worth doing.

5.2 Blogs

In an ideal world, people would automatically know about all the great work that you do. Some sort of cosmic telepathy would spread the word, and affluent customers would line up at your door. Unfortunately, some people think that things really work like that. They think doing good work is all it takes to get a long list of clients. The common claim that "All my business comes from referrals and word of mouth" perpetuates that myth.

Referrals and word of mouth are obviously important, and

the quality of your work needs to be excellent. Relying on your network for new business is likely to be disappointing, though, especially when you are starting out. You simply don't know enough people for your clientele to form a critical mass that creates a steady stream of referrals via chain reaction.

The basic goal of any pull-marketing strategy is to get the word out about what you do. Since the very rich like to do business with experts, the content that you produce and the impression that it makes will have a major impact on how you are perceived. This brings us to your blog. It should go without saying that your blog is a fundamental part of your strategy to become well known for what you do. You will find that your blog can be used in a variety of ways to increase your visibility and reputation among those you most want to do business with.

Let's first discuss what to blog about, and then we'll cover how to make sure people read it. Whenever you have trouble coming up with ideas for content, think about the following questions:

- What *fears* do people have that you help solve?
- What *desires* do they have?
- What are the common *objections* people have to working with you?
- What is the *process* by which people achieve success?

Let's discuss each of these topics in a bit more detail. The first, fear, is very powerful. Remember, people make decisions based on both logic and emotion. Fear is such a powerful attention-grabbing tool because it creates an intense emotion. When one analyzes headlines that garner the most attention, they are usually fear based. News broadcasters have understood this for years, which is why they so often hint at calamity right before going to commercials: "An asteroid is on a collision course with Earth! Will it affect your neighborhood? Details after the break."

What is your prospective client most worried about? According to one study done by the University of Switzerland, the key fears of the rich include: losing power, control or status; losing a sense of life purpose; being anxious for their children; having bad friendships; and not being loved for who they are. Take a moment and think about how your product or service connects with any of these fears. These connections will provide excellent topics for your blog posts.

The flip side of fear is desire. According to one study, the wealthy, perhaps more than other people, have a strong desire to be remembered in a positive way after their death. Author Jason Hornblower recognized this and built a very successful business around this one desire. He says:

> I did a blog about how I had been commissioned to write a biography for a very wealthy gentleman. I discussed in the article that he never wanted to make it available to the general public, but rather it was something he planned on distributing to his children and grandchildren so they would remember him.

> What came as a surprise was the number of wealthy people who reached out to me as a result of that blog who also wanted a "legacy biography" written for them. This has evolved into a rather substantial business over the years. It all had to do with how they wanted future generations to view them.

According to *Financial Times*, other key desires include growing old with dignity, increasing self awareness, and interacting with interesting people. The last point came up repeatedly, so it's worth examining in a bit more detail. What makes a person interesting? Being well versed on a variety of subjects makes one interesting.

What does "interesting" mean in the context of your business? One finding from the study was that while most people know a lot about their own business, they are woefully uninformed about their competitors. Nancy Lang, who says her net worth is "north of $35 million, although I couldn't tell you exactly how far north," tells us:

> One of the things I'm really interested in is the overall state of a particular business segment and how one firm compares to another. I'm really curious about these things and find it disappointing when the person I'm talking to can't talk about trends in their industry and specifics about their competitors.

The lesson here is that you need to be up to date on everything going on in your field. On the surface this would seem obvious, yet in practice it's often overlooked. Psychologist Nancy Sherman explains this phenomenon as follows:

> Since so many people are up to their eyeballs in their business every day, they stop paying attention to what their competitors are doing and as a result miss trends. Just because your day is filled doesn't mean that you're current. There's sort of an intellectual arrogance that sets in, especially for those who have been doing something for a long period of time.

All of this means that you need to make sure that you subscribe to all the relevant trade journals. Get yourself on the mailing lists of your competitors, attend the appropriate conferences, and follow your closest competitors on social media. The wealthy desire conversations with interesting people, and you make yourself interesting by knowing how to have insightful, relevant conversations.

Let's next discuss sourcing blog topics from the list of objections you often hear. The reasons that people choose to not do business with you can provide great content for your blogs. We can start with a universal: money. It's one of the most common reasons you don't get hired, so it's worthwhile to write at least one blog article that addresses this issue. Matt Schulman, a financial advisor in California, says:

> Quite frankly my fees are about twice what a typical advisor would charge. Rather than hide that fact and hope clients don't notice, I actually make it a part of my marketing platform. I've written extensively that in our business you get what you pay for, and as a client, you need to decide whether you want to save a few bucks or avail yourself of world-class advice. Interestingly, a lot of my clients take pride in the fact that they are able to pay my fees.

Similarly, marketer Frank Kern has billed himself as the most expensive copywriter in the world, and he has written extensively about it. Does this title hurt his business? On the contrary, as with Matt Schulman, clients take pride in the fact that they can afford him.

American Express employs a related strategy by attaching high fees to their Platinum and Black cards. I have their Platinum card, but I don't think I really take advantage of the card's benefits. Truth be told, I'm not entirely sure what they are. Ultimately, a credit card is just a credit card. It's a tool for buying stuff. Still, each year I pay the $695 membership fee even though I know I really can't logically justify it.

I will admit that having a metal credit card is pretty cool, but that alone is certainly not worth $695. So why do I pay that fee? I pay it because of the way it makes me feel. I pay it because I like what it says about me. I like that the card fits with the story I tell myself about who I am. Likewise, the rich want to feel different.

They take pride in being able to afford the most expensive services as long as they're given a compelling case for the value they get. Don't overlook this as a topic for your blog.

The fourth and final content theme we'll explore is *process*. Your process for solving client problems can probably be turned into an entire series of blog posts. This topic doesn't just make for interesting reading. Its proper use can provide a highly effective way to convert casual readers into engaged clients.

As I often point out, the easiest way to demonstrate that you can be helpful to clients if they hire you is to be helpful as you're getting to know them. Let's do a little exercise that will help you figure out just how to do that. Take out a piece of paper and draw a sad face on the left side and a happy face on the right. I know this sounds silly, but trust me, this process works.

The sad face represents a client with a problem, and the happy face represents that same client enjoying the results they achieved working with you. Next, draw four or five lines between the two faces. These lines represent the steps your client has to take in order to get from sad to happy. Yes, you're going to oversimplify the process you use to solve client problems, and yes, I know that every client is different. If you've been serving your niche for any length of time, though, you know that there are characteristics that all of your clients share.

The ideas behind the five steps that clients take to move from sad to happy can serve as the starting point for many blog articles. For each step that you've identified, write down some helpful ideas, tips, tactics or strategies that your audience would find valuable. It's possible that you could end up writing a half dozen articles just to share ideas about a single step.

Of course, I know the worry that you probably have. You think, "If I give away all my good ideas for free, they won't want to hire me!" While on the surface this concern might make sense, in reality it represents rather shortsighted thinking. The truth is that there are lots of people who do what you do, and there's a lot of skepticism about whether you can actually do what you say you can do. The way to address both of those issues is to make sure your content provides great value. These blog posts are some of the most powerful and beneficial content you can produce.

Let's now move on to discuss the mechanics of producing your blog. The good news is that it's pretty simple. Adding a blog page to your existing website isn't very complex, and if you need assistance, you can find helpful people on a freelancer website like Upwork or Fiverr.

Publishing a simple blog consisting of nothing but text is entirely fine, although I suggest that you introduce each written post with a short video. As mentioned before, we're borrowing this strategy from Walt Disney. Attaching your face and personality to your content is a powerful and effective brand-building practice. These videos help you seem known, liked, and trusted, and these are key factors for converting wealthy prospects into actual clients.

These videos don't need to be long. Taking two minutes to introduce the content that follows should suffice. Thanks to the videos, however, you can repurpose the blog material in several ways. For example, you can put the video on YouTube and paste the blog content into the video description. You can put the video on Instagram with the content in the title. You can use the videos to promote the blog on LinkedIn, and you can share the content with the LinkedIn groups you belong to. Of course, you can also send your multimedia content directly to your subscribers.

The final piece of the puzzle is a way to turn blog readers into actual clients. One very effective approach is to conclude each blog post with a call to action. For example, at the end of each of my blog articles, I add a postscript that says, "If you are laser-focused on attracting more new affluent clients and you have a reasonable budget for marketing, we should probably talk. Go HERE to arrange that."

The first part of this message defines precisely who I work with. You will adapt it to the niche market you serve. You'll want to think about the primary reason that some people don't do business with you and address that somehow in the second part of the message. In my case, the obstacle is usually money. Quite frankly, if someone doesn't have any money to spend on marketing, I can't be helpful. However, one doesn't need a fortune in order to be successful. That's the reason why I use the word "reasonable."

As you can see, the message I use is highly adaptable for other businesses. The second sentence is the call to action. You will provide the reader with a link that can be used to arrange a conversation, but that's not all. Much like you, I don't have the time to talk with everyone. I'm happy to have people in my business community, but I need to focus my time on those who have the potential to become clients.

For this reason, the link doesn't go directly to my calendar, but rather it takes the reader to a short questionnaire. I use Typeform, but there are many other services you can use. Thanks to the exercises you did earlier in the book, you should have a very clear understanding of who your ideal client is. This information should make it easy to set up a series of screening questions for the questionnaire.

I first ask for basic contact information such as name, email address and phone number. With this I create a record in my database, and the database entries are used to send people my weekly blog content. I make the phone number optional since I've found that if I require it I mostly get fake numbers.

The next thing I ask for is the address of their website. Visiting their site helps me learn about them prior to our conversation and gives me a sense of how sophisticated their marketing is. Does their site make me an offer to induce me to join their community? Is it apparent what types of clients they best serve? Do they have a blog? Such details will prove useful in any future conversation.

I also ask everyone explicitly what kind of work they do. No matter how clearly you specify the types of clients you work with, you'll still get inquiries from outliers. It's very helpful to know who people are before you invest the time to talk with them. Likewise, you want to know how long they've been in business. I ask this, for example, because I'm not the right advisor for someone who is just starting out or who is merely thinking about starting a business.

Next, my questionnaire asks for the average value of their clients. This helps me determine what type of budget they might have for marketing. To give an extreme example, if the value of a client is a dime, you need to bring on a lot of clients to recoup the cost of a $1000 marketing campaign. On the other hand, if an average client is worth $2,000, they only need to win one half of a client to make their money back.

I next ask how much they spend each year on marketing. I like to work with people who are doing at least a little bit of marketing. They don't have to be marketing extensively, and their efforts don't necessarily have to be effective, but I like people who aren't marketing virgins. Knowing this number is beneficial for many businesses that are marketing to the affluent. Obviously, this is key information for me since I'm a marketing consultant.

In addition to knowing something about their marketing activity, I also want to know what they are currently doing to attract new clients. This builds on the last question and provides me with a greater understanding of where they are on the marketing spectrum. You might adapt this question to suit your particular business. For example, a financial advisor could ask for information about the types of investments a prospective client engages in.

Finally, before the person is given the calendar page on which to set a date and time for our conversation, I ask what they would like our conversation to focus on. By letting the prospect set the agenda, you can provide the greatest help to them in the shortest amount of time. Once they've booked a date and time, an automated system can be used to send out reminder messages and reduce the number of no-shows.

The key takeaway here is that a blog can be used to achieve

several goals. It can be invaluable for building your brand and positioning yourself as a recognized expert in your field. If you follow my suggestion to create a new blog post every week, you can stay in touch with your prospects by sharing your new content. Finally, by incorporating into your posts an offer to speak with you personally, you can use your blog to turn passive readers into paying clients.

5.3 Speaking

It's often said that public speaking is one of the activities that people fear the most. On the other hand, there are people who relish the opportunity to speak before a group. If that's you, then speaking can be a highly effective way to increase your visibility among the wealthy. As with any marketing effort, there are a number of factors that will ensure your success, so let's dive in.

First, it's important that you be perceived as an expert. This might seem rather obvious, but many people try to get speaking engagements simply because they happen to do something. As I've said before, simply doing good work isn't enough. You have to be recognized for what you do. If you're serious about speaking anywhere other than the local Rotary or Kiwanis, you need to be known as one of the experts in your field.

Your social media presence can play an important role in your reputation for excellence, and any press coverage you've received can make a big difference as well. Being an author can give you a tremendous amount of credibility, although given that anyone can publish a book these days, that doesn't actually make a whole lot of sense. Writing a book has never been easier, so there's really no excuse not to have written one. Writing your book and then taking the steps necessary to get it to number one in a category on Amazon gives you a type of credibility that outranks all the others. If you're serious about using speaking engagements as a method for gaining visibility, you need to do this.

Assuming you're able to get meaningful speaking engagements, you need to make a good impression. Speaking is about both substance and style. You need to develop your voice, comfort, and a personal way of giving a speech. Interior designer Maggie Rothmore recalls:

> I had taken a few acting classes in high school, and although I knew that becoming an actor wasn't in the cards, the experience did make me very comfortable speaking before a group of people. My personal "style," if you can call it that, is one of empowerment. People often get uncertain when trying to figure out what type of furniture to buy or what colors to paint the wall. As a result they rely on the opinions and style of others, which may be quite different from their own. My talks focus on creating self-confidence in making design decisions, so my style is very exuberant and motivational.

If you're not naturally someone who feels comfortable presenting to a group, consider taking an improv or acting class.

Organizations such as Toastmasters don't just help you develop your speaking skills. Through repetition and practice, they help you develop the confidence that you need to be an effective speaker. Financial advisor Leslie Sherman says:

> I really didn't feel comfortable speaking to a group, but I saw how others in the office had used talks as a very effective method for increasing their visibility. My boss suggested I enroll in an improv class at the local community college. I don't think I ever felt sillier in my life, and to be perfectly honest, I've realized I'm not a very good improv actor. However, much to my pleasant surprise, the class dramatically increased my comfort level when giving a talk. I'm glad I did it.

Obviously, no organizer wants to hire a speaker and then have him or her freeze on stage. You'll need some video shots of you giving presentations so that you can create a sizzle reel. If you are just starting out, have someone record you standing in front of a room giving a presentation. It may come as a surprise, but most people won't catch on to the fact that there isn't an audience. Billy Simmons says:

> When I started out, a buddy and I shot me doing a short presentation in a hotel conference room. It was just me and him there. I did the presentation four

> times wearing different clothes. Then I hired an editor on Upwork to cut the four videos into one. It looked like I had done a number of presentations when in fact I was just starting out. The other advantage of doing this was that I cherry picked the best bits from the presentations, which made the compilation reel look really good.

You'll want to have a page on your website that is devoted to speaking. Your sizzle reel appears at the top, and the rest of the page provides the different topics you can speak about and a summary of each talk. It is quite important that you be able to summarize your talks. If you've ever sat through a talk that went on and on and on and made you ask yourself "What in the world is his point?" then you can appreciate the importance of having a structure for a talk. Most of us just can't get away with winging it.

A common mistake is to load up the presentation with way too much information. Focus instead on between one and three key takeaways. There's a standard three-part structure that has been around since people started giving speeches. You don't have to rigidly adhere to it, but it works surprisingly well, and it's suitable for virtually any presentation.

The structure has you start by telling the audience what you're going to tell them. You basically say, "Thank you for having me here tonight. In our short time together, I'd like to share with you X, Y and Z." Next, you tell them about those three things. You give them a story about each one. Finally, you tell the audience what you have told them. You say something like, "To sum things up, if you take away nothing else from our time together, I would encourage you to remember X, Y and Z."

Naturally, you'll want to adapt this structure to your own personal speaking style. Just remember that stories are the lifeblood of any good presentation, so the more you can illustrate your points with interesting anecdotes, the better. Also, although you obviously need to know a lot about the minutiae of your topic, it's important that you can speak about the larger trends. Maggie Rothmore says:

> One adjustment I had to make when I started giving talks was not to get too focused on the details. What people were most interested in were the big picture things that are shaping interior design. The topic of color trends provides one of the highlights of my talks, and it's the one that people ask me to speak about the most.

Let's talk now about exactly how to get speaking gigs. The first and most obvious step is to figure out where you want to speak. Think back to the ideal candidate profile that you prepared earlier. What groups or organizations would they likely be members of? Searching for relevant conferences to speak at is pretty simple. Let's say you want to speak to owners of automobile dealerships. Simply go to Google and search for "Automobile dealer conferences."

The large national conferences will appear at the top of page one, but don't stop there. Scroll down and look for smaller or local conferences. These are the ones that are usually hungriest for interesting speakers. An advanced tip is to scroll all the way to the bottom of the page until you see the section called "Searches related to (your subject)." This section will provide you with associated keywords that you'll want to enter into the search bar. Do this same exercise again with those related keywords.

You can also find speaking opportunities on Facebook, Twitter, Instagram and LinkedIn. Search with hashtags such as #conference, #events, #conferencespeaker or #businessevent. This pulls up not only events but also people that are worth connecting with. A large percentage of speaking opportunities are filled through word of mouth, so the more you are a part of the network, the more opportunities you'll hear about.

It's also a good idea to attend the events that you would like to speak at, and when you're there, make sure you take a lot of selfies and photos and post them on all the social media channels. The first thing conference organizers do after their event is search for it on social media, and when they enter the conference hashtag, your photos will pop up. Enhancing your visibility and associating yourself with their events in this way will make it seem natural that you might get more involved.

Social media follow-up is also a great time to tell the organizers how much you enjoyed the event. Tell them that you hope your promoting it on your social channels was helpful. They'll love to hear from you, and this is an opportune time to mention that you would like to be considered as a speaker the following year.

You can also use third-party websites to list your availability for speaking engagements. Registration with GigSalad.com and Thumbtack are both worthwhile. Having gone this far, some people also wonder if speaker's bureaus are worth trying. You can think of speaker's bureaus as agents that represent you to associations and other groups that are looking to book speakers. The good news is that their services are free, so there is no downside to registering with as many as will take you. Unfortunately, unless you're a celebrity, speaker's bureaus most likely won't generate much activity for you, so don't expect much.

Once you've created a list of relevant events, visit the websites to learn when they take speaker applications. Requests for presenters at national and regional conferences usually go out a year in advance. In your pitch letter to the event coordinator, you need to present your topic with their perspective in mind. Why would it be interesting to their audience? What will they learn or how will they benefit from your talk?

Celebrities can get away with just showing up and talking about whatever they want, but you need to make the reasons for inviting you to speak readily apparent. One effective way to do this is to summarize the major points you plan on making in your talk. For each of these, explicitly say why the audience will care about it and what they will learn from it.

What will get the most attention from a selection committee is a contrarian position or an adversarial opinion. Is there any prevailing wisdom that you think is just plain wrong? What are people usually failing to consider when they make a decision in your area of expertise? What overlooked factor often makes the difference between success and failure in your industry?

You get the idea. Be a bit controversial or a little bit contrary. For example, my book *The One Week Marketing Plan* led to a series of speaking opportunities because its premise was that most people make marketing way too complicated, time consuming and expensive. I discussed a way for any business to get a highly effective marketing system up and running in as little as seven days. That was a great hook, and it generated a lot of curiosity and interest.

Determine what your most compelling pitch is and email or snail mail it (or both) to the relevant person in the association. That individual can usually be found by calling the association office and asking who is responsible for selecting speakers for the next meeting. Associations are interested in putting on a great event, so there is usually a well established process for applying. Make sure that you customize each pitch to the person and the event that you are applying to. Nothing turns off event coordinators more than a cut-and-paste presentation.

Follow up a few days after you've sent your pitch, and if you don't hear anything after another week, follow up again. If you still don't hear anything, try one last time thirty days prior to the event. Conferences often have scheduled speakers back out at the last minute for one reason or another. Mention that while you know they have most likely filled their speaker positions, in the event that someone cancels at the last moment, you are available to fill in. If nothing else, this will be seen as a nice offer on your part, and it will generate some good will that might make a difference when you apply for the following year's conference.

Ultimately, the best way to get the speaking engagements you most want is to start small and work your way up the food chain. Although it sounds obvious, showing up on time, being prepared and doing a great job will build your reputation as someone worth hiring. The world of professional speaking is filled with prima-donnas, so being competent and nice goes a long way.

5.4 Social media

One of the most significant changes in marketing over the past several decades has been the rise of social media. From chatting to dating to sharing videos on TikTok, social media has fundamentally changed how people interact. A belief long held by many business people was that high-net-worth individuals did not use social media. I have no idea how this erroneous assumption gained a foothold.

Certainly the affluent use social media differently than the masses do. They are far more circumspect about posting due to security concerns, but a 2020 Spectrum study found that 69% of ultra-high-net-worth investors (those with a net worth between five and twenty-five million dollars not counting their primary residence) use social media. Where do the wealthy go online, and what are some strategies you should consider to connect with them?

The first platform to consider is Facebook. Interestingly, Facebook can work as a part of your affluent marketing strategy, but probably not in the way you think. The affluent client you want to do business with is most likely not on Facebook, but his or her children, parents and relatives may be. The question thus becomes what are they interested in, curious about, or concerned with? What might you be able to assist these associated people with?

One campaign my agency helped set up focused on common issues faced by children of the wealthy. For example, how do they know whether people like them for who they are or because of how much money they have? What's the etiquette when one person in the group can afford social activities that are a stretch for the others?

Such questions related to the "socialization of wealth" are of significant interest and importance to the extremely affluent and their children. Helpful advice disseminated through Facebook posts enabled my client to develop relationships not only with the children of the wealthy but also with their parents. Over time, this approach became a significant tool for building important new relationships.

A similar approach can be used on Instagram. For one client, a series of humorous videos depicting social "calamities" provided an effective way to initiate connections. Keep in mind that Instagram has its own vibe, and you need to use it consistently and in a highly engaging manner. We've established Instagram programs for cosmetic dentists, financial advisors and attorneys, and these programs have been very effective for building the clients' personal brands.

It can be correctly argued that YouTube is less of a social

media channel than it is a search engine, but there is no denying its considerable power for relationship building. For clients including wealth managers, cosmetic surgeons and aircraft leasing companies, we have developed a strategy that uses YouTube in an educational way. Whether you post talking-head-style videos or elaborate mini-movies, YouTube is a valuable tool for building trust and credibility.

LinkedIn is by far the most commonly used social media platform among high-net-worth individuals. The good news is that your best clients and prospects are on LinkedIn. The bad news is that LinkedIn doesn't make it easy to market your services to them. There are severe limits on how many connection requests you can make per day, week and month. There are also limits on how many messages you can send to those who are in your network. Do the restrictions mean that you should pass on using LinkedIn for marketing? Not at all, but you have to be willing to take some additional steps in your efforts. We'll take a look at a couple of strategies that are worth considering.

First, LinkedIn groups can be a highly effective way to get your content in front of a narrowly targeted group of prospective clients. Most groups don't want you to overtly promote your services, so using your blog content as the bait to get prospects to your website is a preferred tactic. Keep in mind that although a group may have thousands of members, only a very small percentage of them are active on any given day. Making this strategy work requires consistently publishing content.

LinkedIn can also be a very effective tool for conducting

research on people and for making highly personalized overtures. You're likely to make several attempts before receiving a positive response, but it can definitely be worth the effort. A key point is that you need to develop a specific reason for why you want to connect. Obviously you should avoid making blatant pitches or using any of the cliched connection requests. Planning and creativity are crucial to making this work.

Since LinkedIn makes it so difficult to communicate with your prospects on a regular basis, your strategy should be to migrate your LinkedIn connections to your personal subscriber list. This may sound complicated, but it's really not. You can do it by following two simple steps.

The first step is to increase your number of connections. You do this by making posts to relevant groups and by directly reaching out to those that you feel would be excellent prospects. There isn't a great way to automate this, so you'll need to either set aside time each day to send connection requests or outsource the work. This is actually one of the services we offer with our *Done For You* program, and you can reach out via our website www.GentleRainMarketing.com to discuss the details.

The second step is, of course, to migrate your connections from LinkedIn to your own subscriber list. This is important because regularly communicating with your prospects is crucial for building trust and credibility. LinkedIn is great for identifying excellent prospects, but it's lousy for ongoing communication. You need to migrate them off of LinkedIn as quickly as possible. Getting them to opt in to receiving emails from you can mean the difference between success and failure.

In order to migrate your prospects, you need to provide them with a reason to visit your website. Once they visit your site, you need to provide them a reason to opt in and become part of your community. The lead magnet or free offer is the catalyst that makes this happen. It could be a free report, a white paper, a survey result, a video, or something else. Whatever it is, it needs to address something that your targeted niche market has great curiosity about. It needs to be something your prospects will have an interest in getting.

In our case, I offer a free copy of my book *Unique Sales Stories*. In fact, many of you reading this came to be a part of my community as a result of that offer. This is a great free offer for me to make since I know that my audience is interested in building their business brand, and I know that stories are a powerful tool for doing that.

Keep in mind that when you offer high value services, it will take time to build credibility and trust. I've been in this business for thirty years, and the typical prospect is usually on my list for between three and six months before they finally decide to talk with me. In one instance, a client was on my list for three years before they decided to take action.

I'm not suggesting that it will take this long for your prospects to take action. There are a lot of variables in play. I am suggesting, though, that in order for your marketing system to provide real results, you need to be communicating with your prospects on a very consistent basis. It is extremely important that you take the long-game approach to this. One post will get you virtually nothing, but consistent, creative work properly tailored for each platform can yield a surprising number of relationships with extremely wealthy individuals.

A strong presence on social media also pays dividends aside from helping you directly connect with clients. For example, if you want to give a speech before a group, one of the first things a conference organizer will do is check out the number of connections you have on social media. Likewise, if you pitch a book idea to a mainstream publisher, one of the first things they will do is check you out on social media.

Along with many others, the people who book speakers and who publish books will use your social media presence to gauge how well respected you are for your expertise. Obviously, conclusions drawn from a review of social media are going to conflate quantity with quality, but that's just part of the game. One of your overarching goals when marketing to the affluent is to be perceived as an expert, and to achieve this, you need a robust social media posting schedule. Even if it sometimes doesn't seem to be worth the effort, enhancing your visibility in this way is a key part of your overall strategy.

5.5 Advertising

Let's turn our attention to the last component of the pull-marketing strategy: advertising. Does advertising work when marketing to the affluent? According to research done by Wealth Management.com, the answer is "Yes, sort of."

Instagram ads don't tend to attract ultra-high-net-worth prospects, but this is primarily due to the average age of its users. As a social media platform matures, the average age of its users increases. While Instagram might not be a viable advertising option at the time I'm writing this book, that might change in the future.

Facebook is a case in point. According to a recent study done by Pew Research Center, Facebook use in the U.S. has increased the most among those aged 65 or older. 65% of this population now uses the app regularly compared to just 26% a few years ago. Likewise, a survey of 1300 millionaires conducted by Spectrum Group showed that 57% of that population now uses Facebook regularly. The survey suggests that LinkedIn is currently the second most popular social media app among millionaires.

While social media advertising can be effective, if you are focused on prospects with a very high net worth, print advertising may offer a better return than digital. It might be worth considering print publications that target the wealthy such as *Robb Report*, *Tatler*, *Elite Traveler*, and *Departures*. The "How To Spend It" section of *Financial Times* might also be promising.

Whether online or off, your results will be substantially better if you incorporate direct response marketing principles rather than relying solely on image ads. What's the difference? Image ads are heavily used by many luxury manufacturers, and their aims are to reinforce brand associations and to elicit certain feelings. This can work well for fashion, cologne and jewelry, but it is very difficult to determine the effectiveness of such ads.

Imagine you run an image ad and soon after get five calls from prospective clients. You could ask them how they heard about you, but people's memories are notoriously imprecise. You'll have a hard time determining whether those clients came as a result of the ad, some other promotional activities you're doing, word of mouth, a Google search, or something else entirely.

Image ads often work without much conscious awareness by the reader. The people who sell advertising will argue that this is a part of why they're so good for building your brand. While they have a point, I feel strongly that you want to be able to track the effectiveness of your advertising. This is why I recommend direct-response advertising.

Direct-response ads focus on a call to action. They are designed to motivate people to do something like call a number, scan a hashtag, or visit a website. The motivation to take action usually involves the offer of some sort of information that they will find valuable. This offer is often called the "hook," and it usually addresses something that the target market wants to achieve or wants to avoid.

Earlier in the book, you did a series of exercises to identify your ideal client. As a part of that exercise, you compiled lists of the things that this client wants to achieve or avoid. Now would be a good time to refresh your memory about what you wrote down. This material will be used to create your advertising campaign.

Earlier we mentioned the twin levers of marketing, pain and gain, and we noted that pain tends to grab people's attention a bit more. Rather than running an ad featuring the name of your company and a tagline, I suggest focusing your ad on one of your prospects' pain points. For example, estate attorney Kevin Shambortz knew that his clients struggled to discuss their wealth with their children. He says:

> I wrote an article about the six things you need to do before discussing inheritances with your children. I ran an ad in *Robb Report* and *Financial Times* that promoted the report and directed people to a website to download it. I also ran some ads on Facebook.
>
> I had tried more traditional advertising with the name of the firm and our logo previously but was frustrated that I didn't know how successful it was. This way I could track both cost per lead and the cost to acquire a new client. For example, I discovered that although Facebook generated a lot of leads, hardly any of them converted into actual clients. The ad in *Financial Times* pulled significantly fewer requests for the free report, but the conversion rate was excellent. That ad more than paid for itself.
>
> This also enabled me to test different ads. I started with the six things you need to do but then tested the reverse of that pitch with the ad headline "6 Mistakes Wealthy Parents Make When Discussing Money With Their Kids." That pulled twice the number of responses. I followed that up with an ad headline that said "Don't Raise Financially Spoiled Brats–What

> You Need to Know Before Talking With Your Kids About Money." That ad pulled the largest number of requests, but similar to my Facebook ads, hardly anyone converted into clients. The second ad generated less initial interest but had a far better return on investment. I wouldn't have been able to know any of this if the ads did not have a very specific call to action.

The first step in developing your advertising campaign is to determine what type of offer you want to make. That's what you promote in your ad. The key is to make sure that whatever you offer will make your target audience sufficiently curious. You'll pique their curiosity with the headline.

The headline is where you tell your prospects about the pain you can relieve for them or the benefit you can offer them. It's arguably the most important part of the ad since if you don't hook them with the headline, they're unlikely to read the rest of the copy, and your chances of getting them to opt in will be significantly reduced. Conversely, if you create a really great headline, you can sometimes get a lot of new subscribers from that alone.

If your free report has a great title, the title itself might be a suitable headline. For example, let's say your free offer is called "7 Secrets to Buying Great Homes for Bargain Prices in Any Real Estate Market." That title would probably look great in large print across the top of the page. One additional word might create a slightly more powerful headline: "FREE: 7 Secrets to Buying

Great Homes for Bargain Prices in Any Real Estate Market."

Alternatively, you might want to look at some of the headline templates we covered in the last chapter and create something new. Sometimes I come up with a few different headlines while writing a free report. The ones I don't use often are repurposed on the website or as bullet points.

In addition to social media and print advertising, anyone undertaking a modern ad campaign has to consider advertising on Google. When you perform a Google search, you get two kinds of results: organic search results and paid advertisements. Ads appear at the top of the page and the organic search results follow. Where and how often an ad appears on the search results page depends on how much the advertiser said they're willing to pay for each click and on what percentage of people who view the ad actually click on it. The more people click on an ad and the more the advertiser pays Google per click, the more prominently the ad is displayed.

The first step in creating a Google ad is to select the keywords or keyword phrases for your campaign. Ask yourself what your prospective client might type into the search box if they were seeking your services or trying to solve a problem. For example, an estate planning attorney might use "estate planning," "estate planning lawyer," "estate planning attorney," "wills" and "trusts."

There are many resources available online that can help you create a list of keywords. My personal favorite is Publisher Rocket. It can easily generate a long list of keywords related to a chosen topic, and it is helpful not only for advertising on Google but also for your Amazon book marketing campaign. (Yes, once again I am urging you to write a book.)

Once you've created a list of keywords, you can refine it using Google's Keyword Planner. This tool will give you information such as the average number of monthly searches for a term, how much material already exists that is associated with a keyword, and the average CPC (cost-per-click) for ads featuring a keyword. Of course, you're hoping to find keywords that are relevant to your work, that lots of people are searching for, and that nobody is currently using in their ads.

Creating a Google Adwords account is quite straightforward. At the time of this writing, you simply go to http://www.google.com/adwords and click "Get started" at the top of the page. If you follow the step-by-step instructions that appear next, you'll have your account set up, active and ready to use in less than an hour.

Creating ads in Google is also pretty simple. There is currently a twenty-five-character limit for your ad headline, and you can use up to seventy characters in the body of the ad. You can satisfy these constraints and maximize the impact of your ad by following the formula I give below. This approach is not just effective in Google, either. You can use it for banner ads that appear on relevant blogs, websites or news publications.

First, make sure to include one of your keywords in the title. People find you because they searched for a particular keyword, and they feel more comfortable clicking when your headline contains the word they were searching for. Second, focus on benefits rather than features. Remember the difference: a feature is what a thing is, while a benefit is what that thing will do for you. Since you only have ninety-five characters with which to convince people to click, focus on benefits.

The more you appeal to the basic question that is running through the prospect's mind, the more effective your ad will be. People will respond to your ad if they believe your free offer will give them something that's important to them. For example, "personal injury attorney" is one of the most expensive keyword phrases at an average cost of $47 per click. These firms can't afford not to have their ads convert, so they make compelling offers such as "Find out how much your case may be worth." Likewise, a realtor who offers a free report on recent sales in a particular neighborhood might use the phrase "Find out how much your house is worth."

When it comes to writing your headline, remember that its purpose is to grab people's attention. If an estate planning lawyer is creating an ad, they'll want the keyword phrase "estate planning" in the headline since that's what people will be typing in the search box. Since "estate planning" and the space after it will require sixteen characters, there will be only nine characters left to work with. They might use the catchy word "secrets," which has only seven characters and is likely to motivate people to read the next line in the ad. A great headline for the estate planning lawyer is thus "Estate Planning Secrets."

The text that follows the lawyer's headline will highlight the benefits on offer. In the case of estate planning, perhaps the two biggest benefits are cost cutting and tax reduction. The body of the ad should mention both since some people want more affordable estate planning while others are more concerned about reducing the inheritance tax liability for their heirs. The next line in the ad might then read "Lower your costs and their taxes."

At this point, they'd have thirty-six characters left to tell readers what they're going to get and what they're going to have to do to get it. A mention of the free report and a call to action might look something like "Click now for the free report." To complete the ad they would input a "Display URL," and their finished product would appear as follows:

Estate Planning Secrets
Lower your costs and their taxes.
Click now for the free report.
www.BillyBobLegal.com

You can use this as a model for advertising on Facebook and LinkedIn as well. The use of such ads can be quite effective for attracting new affluent clients. Just remember what you're trying to do. You are using the ad to motivate prospects to raise their hands. They express an initial interest in receiving your free offer, and then you follow up effectively as described in this book.

Chapter 6:
Push marketing

Let's now shift our attention to push marketing. As the name implies, this type of marketing involves pushing your offer onto prospects. You do this with the hope of convincing them that you have something they want before they hang up, delete your email or throw away your letter. The classic example of push marketing is cold calling.

Does cold calling work? Sure, but it has a lot of downsides. It's labor intensive, it's not a whole lot of fun, and you get lots and lots of rejections. It does have a few upsides. For example, it doesn't cost much to implement, and it doesn't take much time or thought. Unfortunately, this often just turns it into a way to keep busy for people who confuse activity with productivity and who have a lot of time on their hands. But who knows? Maybe it will lead to something.

I'll admit up front that I have a bias. While push marketing can work, it usually takes an extremely high level of persistence for it to bear fruit, especially if you are focused on the affluent market. Personally, I would recommend that you focus your efforts on connecting to the wealthy by using the methods we've discussed in the previous chapters. If you don't find success building relationships by attending events, symposiums and other activities frequented by the wealthy, then I would turn my efforts towards doing what needs to be done to become one of the recognized experts in your field.

In the spirit of providing you with a comprehensive guide to all of the available tools, however, I'll be covering in this chapter direct mail, email marketing, and everyone's least favorite activity: cold calling. Among the strategies I'm going to discuss, direct mail has the greatest likelihood of success, but we will begin this chapter with some advice about your website.

6.1 What type of website do you need?

I suppose the first question is "Do you really need a website?" The answer is a resounding yes. At a minimum, you need a brochure-style website so that prospective clients can look you up and check you out. However, while a brochure website might be sufficient for establishing credibility, it won't do much to help you attract new business. That is, it won't help you unless we at least tweak it a bit.

The primary problem with brochure websites is that prospects visit the site and then leave without letting you know that they were there. Obviously, it's difficult to stay in touch with people if you don't know who they are, and, as you know, staying in touch and nurturing your relationships are crucially important when marketing to the wealthy.

Our prospective clients are skeptical. Some don't think they need our services while others are already working with one of our competitors. You therefore have three goals for your website: establish credibility, capture contact information so you can stay in touch, and motivate prospects to arrange a conversation with you. Your site can accomplish these goals if its design focuses on a few key elements. Let's talk about how precisely to do this.

The first element is the welcome. The goal of the welcome is to make visitors feel that they have finally found a place that focuses on them. Sure, they'll be interested in you and your expertise, but in the beginning, if you want them to stick around and engage with you, you need to focus on them and what they are interested in.

The first part of the welcome is the headline that people see when they first arrive at the page. It should call out to the people that you are trying to attract, and it should reference a particular problem that they are facing. It might say something like:

- Tested Real World Investment Advice for Successful Small Business Owners
- Bespoke Concierge Medical Services for Discerning Couples and Individuals
- Turnkey Luxury Interior Design for Discerning Miami Residents
- Digital Security for High-Net-Worth Families
- Collectable Cars for Enthusiasts and Investors

- Shaping Financial Legacies for Ultra-High-Net-Worth Individuals and Their Families

The second part of the welcome is a video. Nothing builds credibility and makes people feel like they know, like and trust you quite as much as a video. If you're not comfortable in front of a camera, you can use a narrated PowerPoint or Keynote presentation. Yet another option is to create a short video that conveys the essence of your products or services. You can find great creative talent to put together a thirty-second video if you search a freelance site like Upwork. However, if you provide personal or professional services, I highly recommend a short video that features you. It doesn't have to be elaborate. A simple talking-head-style video is more than adequate.

My suggestion for what to say in your video is to simply welcome them to your site and thank them for visiting. After that opening, you might say something like "While I have you here, allow me to give you a quick tour of the site. I think there are a number of resources here that you will find interesting and helpful." If you would like to see a complete introductory presentation that is easily adaptable for any business, go to www.GentleRainMarketing.com.

A slightly different approach for the video is to use it to encourage people to download your free offer. I've found that using the video in this way does increase the percentage of people who opt in. If you want to try this approach to your video, here's a script you can use:

> Welcome! I'm glad that you're here. If you're like most of my visitors, you're probably frustrated by (a particular challenge or problem). That's why I created (the title of your free offer). In this report you'll discover (the top two or three benefits of the report). So what I'd like you to do is fill out your name and email address and click on the button below. You'll immediately receive an email with a link to download your free report. Again, thanks very much for visiting my site. I'm sure you'll find reviewing (name of report) to be a good investment of your time.

Some people like to watch videos, some like to read, and some like to do both, so the next website element to focus on is the supporting text. This is the copy that follows the video, and it mostly covers the same ground. In it you can elaborate on the problem you solve and perhaps provide a bit more detail about what others are doing to address the issue.

Remember when writing the supporting text that the best way to show that you can be of service to someone when they hire you is to provide real value in your marketing material. Also remember that lead magnets often succeed or fail because of how "hooky" the title is. As we discussed earlier, you want to focus on a pain point or play strongly on the curiosity of your target audience.

The majority of your affluent clients will probably come from your subscriber list as opposed to signing on after their initial visit to your site. The more you sell high-value products or services, the more this is true. Thus, always keep in mind that mission one is to get website visitors to tell you who they are so that you can stay in contact with them.

In addition to building credibility and getting contact information about who is visiting your site, another important role of your website is to facilitate an exploratory conversation between you and your affluent prospect. As we've touched on repeatedly, when marketing to the wealthy, a relationship usually needs to be in place *before* prospects become paying clients, and a free consultation helps greatly in this regard.

This offer is something most people don't get right. A simple form that says "Sign up for a free consultation" isn't going to be enough. Even though it's free, you need to emphasize the benefits and sell the prospect on taking time out of their day to speak with you. The more specific, beneficial outcomes you can promise from your meeting, the better.

To help clarify what's in it for them, think about the metaphorical journey your client needs to go on if they are to achieve their goals. There will be certain obstacles and milestones along the way. In the consultation, you want to offer insight and perspective, and you want to tell them how to achieve success at each step. Alternatively, you could provide a high-level blueprint about what others in your industry are doing to solve a particular problem.

Since I live in the world of marketing, my free consultation could include a variety of things. I might review their website, critique their latest marketing campaign, suggest topics for their free report, or describe what goes into a successful client-attraction marketing system. You get the idea. The point is just that your offer of a free consultation needs to communicate the value that people will get from speaking with you.

Probably the easiest way to reassure people that the free consultation won't just be a sales pitch in disguise is to make sure that all of your marketing material offers helpful tips, tactics, ideas and suggestions. If you have a history of being helpful, the resistance to scheduling a free consultation will be dramatically reduced.

You need to be careful, though, about giving away your time. While the goal is to get lots of people to want to talk with you, you need to be very selective about who you spend time with. As mentioned earlier, make sure to include a short questionnaire for people to complete before you meet. Think about the profile of your ideal client to figure out what to ask, and think about what's most important to you. Relevant details might be things like the size of their company or what kind of marketing budget they have.

I've outlined the steps, but how does this all work in practice? It's actually not hard at all. You just need to add a page to your website. This page will be set up to accomplish three things. First, it will sell prospects on the benefits of the free consultation. Second, it will provide the questionnaire so that you can focus on those who can afford you and that you want to work with. Third, it will provide the means to schedule the free consultation.

As a reality check, note that the odds of a first-time visitor signing up for a free consultation are low. I cannot emphasize enough that the mindset of the affluent prospect is one of skepticism. They may be slightly intrigued by you and what you offer, but that's rarely enough to create a willingness to take time out of their day to talk with you. This is why staying in touch is crucially important.

You understand that you need to send messages and keep in touch, but what should you communicate with these messages? I suggest that you prepare an initial sequence of email messages that go out after the prospect has opted in for your free report, video or other lead magnet. What follows is a sequence that I recommend you use. At the end of each message, in the P.S., remind them of the free consultation offer and provide a link to the page.

- Message 1: Send the link so that they can download your free report.
- Message 2: Send a quick follow up to make sure they received the first email. Make sure you include the link to access the free information again.
- Message 3: Ask them if they found the information helpful. This is a highly effective way to motivate those who have not yet read the report to do so.
- Message 4: Tell a story about how someone is using the advice you shared. You don't need to mention a specific name or company. Just communicate that people like them have solved their problems by following your advice.

- Message 5: Offer an additional tip or idea that was not included in the report.
- Message 6: Answer a question that a client asked you recently. (If you don't have clients yet, you can just think of a question that prospective clients would likely ask.)

I would send Message 2 the day after they downloaded the report and send each of the others about forty-eight hours apart. Although this might seem too frequent, the reality is that you are just one message in a constant stream of communications. You want to cement in their minds as quickly as possible who you are and what you do.

After the initial sequence has been delivered, your weekly blog entries can provide the basis for your ongoing communication. At the end of each blog article, add a P.S. that identifies the types of people you work with and suggest that they should reach out for a conversation. My long-serving and highly effective P.S. is "If you want to attract more affluent clients and have a reasonable budget for marketing, we should talk. Go HERE to arrange that conversation." The HERE is a hyperlink to my website www.GentleRainMarketing.com.

By following these suggestions, you can easily create a website that builds credibility for you, grows your community of prospective affluent clients, and facilitates one-on-one conversations.

6.2 Direct mail

The suggestion to use direct mail may come as a surprise. After all, who actually sends letters these days? I think it is a universal hope that when we go to the mailbox we will find something interesting. The fact that practically no one sends letters is precisely why you don't want to overlook direct mail as a marketing tool.

When properly constructed, a tangible letter addressed personally to a prospect or client conveys a level of elegance and quality that an email or text never can. Direct mail also enables you to micro-target your marketing efforts. In one sense, marketing is all about reducing waste. You want to avoid trying to sell to people who will never do business with you. The beauty of direct mail is that if you buy the right mailing list, you'll only be sending personal correspondence to the affluent prospects who are most likely to be interested in what you're offering.

There are different types of mailing lists, but I encourage you to focus on what is called a "response list." These are lists of people who have signaled with their previous buying behavior that they are a member of some group. For example, it is particularly helpful to know what magazines your target audience subscribes to. If I subscribe to *Cigar Aficionado*, it's likely that I'm interested in travel, gambling and golf. If I subscribe to *Departures*, then I'm likely quite wealthy, and I likely enjoy travel. If I subscribe to *Financial Times* or *Barron's*, I'm probably a sophisticated investor who keeps current on global issues.

As a general rule, response lists will generate more inquiries. Although they are more expensive than lists that only target zip codes or basic demographics, if your budget allows for it, I'd try to use them as much as possible. There are numerous list brokers from whom you can order mailing lists. INFOUSA is the largest, but I would shop around since deals can often be found.

Once you have a list of potential recipients, it's time to write your letter. You can follow a process similar to the one we used to create your free report or other lead magnet. Just remember that your sales letter needs to initially focus on your reader and not on you and the services you offer. You want to hook their interest and tap into emotional triggers. A sales letter that mentions what they desire and what they are afraid of will get read and acted on. Those that don't will get dismissed.

The fear of pain and the desire for gain are the most powerful motivators available for moving your prospects to take the actions that you want. While the desire for gain is effective, the fear of pain is much better at grabbing people's attention, so that's what you want to focus on. This can be effectively done through a simple process.

First, you want to express a problem that your readers are facing. When marketing to the affluent, you can also highlight issues faced by those associated with them. Just stating the problem is usually not enough, however. You need to build on it. Make your readers care strongly enough about it that they become willing to take action. To do that, you need to present consequences, which are simply the answers to "What happens if this problem isn't addressed?"

The first sentence in your letter has two important objectives.

First off, as the legendary copywriter John Caples puts it, "The goal of the first sentence is simply to get the reader to read the second sentence." Second, I would suggest that not only should it hook the reader's attention, but it should also communicate the credibility of the writer.

The following opening-sentence template accomplishes both objectives and has worked extremely well for my clients:

> Dear (Prospect),
> I know from speaking with (others in the niche) that many of them are concerned about (a problem).

What is interesting about this opening sentence is that it not only gets the prospect's attention, but it also seems to increase the odds that the letter gets past the secretary or screener and into the hands of the decision maker. The reason for this is that it very clearly articulates that you are someone who 1) focuses on people like the reader and 2) apparently has the ear of other wealthy individuals.

Make sure the first sentence appears as a single paragraph. This makes it easier for the eye to focus on it, which increases the likelihood that it will be read. It also makes it more likely that the reader will continue on to the next sentence, and that's key. According to *Direct Marketing News*, if we can get people to read the second paragraph, we have an excellent chance of getting them down the slippery slope of reading the entire message.

I'll give you an example of what this all looks like in an illustrative three-letter sequence later in this chapter, but for now, let's continue with the next part of the letter: your offer. Remember that the whole point of the sales letter is to get readers to visit your website and request the free report. This differs from the offer in a traditional sales letter, which typically encourages the reader to call for more information or to set up a call.

Unfortunately, asking someone to call to speak with you usually doesn't generate much of a response these days. It is simply too big of a request this early in the relationship. You should always make a soft offer when attracting new prospects. You want to make it easy for them to say yes.

Although you've caught their attention by focusing on fear and pain, you can't just dwell on that. Your letter needs a credibility statement. You have to make readers feel comfortable and confident that you have the skills necessary to solve their problems. Interestingly, you will establish a lot of credibility by simply demonstrating that you understand their specific problems. However, you will need to add just a bit more.

What you emphasize in the letter will depend on what you think would be most impressive to your niche audience. This might include your education, special training or how long you have worked in the field. If you've written any articles or books on your subject of expertise, this is often worth mentioning. One way to think about this is to ask yourself "Why don't clients hire me?" The more you can address those issues in your credibility statement and elsewhere in your sales copy, the more you will proactively defuse rejection.

Having constructed the body of your letter, it's time to consider the power of the P.S. A lot of research suggests that a postscript is the part of a sales letter most often read other than the opening sentence. This is where you want to reiterate the call to action or the offer you are making. In tests we've run, repeating the call-to-action in the P.S. has increased response rates by as much as 33%!

We have also found that having three letters in your sequence optimizes the response rate when marketing to the affluent. Our clients have seen as much as an 85% increase compared to sending just one letter. I'd recommend sending the three letters at two-week intervals. Make sure to track who has responded and remove their names from subsequent mailing lists.

Following is a sequence of three letter templates appropriate for most businesses.

Letter 1:

Dear (first name),

I know from speaking with (others in their niche) that many of them are concerned about (a problem). It's an understandable concern since (biggest consequence) can often occur. In fact, we've notice that within (niche field) it's very common to observe the following:

- Consequence 1

- Consequence 2
- Consequence 3

That's why I thought our latest publication (name of your free report) would be of interest to you. This report will take you less than fifteen minutes to read, and in that time you will learn:

- Benefit 1
- Benefit 2
- Benefit 3

At (your company name), we specialize in assisting (niche market) (solve their biggest problem). My personal background includes (mention years of experience working with niche clients and drop names or mention awards and publications if appropriate).

I guarantee that you will find useful and profitable information in (name of your report) and that you'll put it down with new ideas and perspectives. It's free, and you can receive your copy by visiting our website (your website address) or by calling (your phone number).

Thanks for investing your time in reading this letter, and I look forward to hearing from you soon.

Best Regards,

(your name)

P.S. If (solving the particular problem) is mission critical for you, I hope you'll take advantage of the information that's available for free at (your web address). Thanks.

Letter 2:

Dear (first name),

Back in (month you sent Letter 1), I sent you a letter offering a copy of our latest free report (name of free report).

Amid all the mail you get on a typical day, perhaps my letter got overlooked, or maybe you were just too busy at the time to respond. However, since we specialize in working with (niche market), I wanted to write to you again. I firmly believe that the information in the report will be particularly valuable to you.

I know from speaking with others (in the niche market) that ideas for (solving the problem) are likely to be very important to you. (Name of report) will take you less than fifteen minutes to read, and I guarantee it will stimulate your thinking about:

- Specific benefit 1

- Specific benefit 2
- Specific benefit 3

At (your company name), we specialize in assisting (niche market) (solve biggest problem). My personal background includes (mention years of experience working with niche clients and drop names or mention awards and publications if appropriate).

Again, the report is free, and you can receive your copy by visiting our website (your website address) or by calling us at (your phone number). Thanks again.

Best regards,
(your name)
(your title)

P.S. If (solving the particular problem) is mission critical for you, I hope you'll take advantage of the information that's available for free at (your website address). Thanks.

Letter 3:

Dear (first name),

Consider two (individuals of the type you're writing to), both (similar in specific ways), both trying to (accomplish a particular task). One (individual) chugs along at an okay pace, but the nagging feeling that "We could be doing better" never quite goes away. In contrast, the second (individual) continues to (achieve a particular result). Why is one (individual) so successful and the other so average?

We believe that a large part of the answer revolves around the power and potential of (the type of work your company does). When you dig down and really examine what accounts for the success of (these types of people), a key differentiator is (how they effectively utilize or implement a particular solution). The bottom line is that the right type of (solutions) can give you an enormous competitive advantage over your rivals, both big and small.

That's the reason I felt compelled to write to you this last time to make you a final offer of our free report (name of your report). The report will take you less than fifteen minutes to read, and it will stimulate your thinking about:

- What you should be doing to (achieve a particular solution)
- How to zero in on what's probably making your (current solution) needlessly (expensive

or ineffective)

- The most important factor to focus on during any (occurrence that's likely)
- What the most progressive (companies in this industry) are doing to drive new business results

At (your company), we help (individuals) (accomplish a specific goal). Even if you're completely satisfied with your current (approach to the particular problem), I guarantee that you will find some useful and profitable information in this report. It's free, and you can receive your copy by visiting our website (your website address) or by calling us at (your phone number). I look forward to hearing from you.

Best regards,
(your name)
(your title)

P.S. If (solving the particular problem) is mission critical for you, I hope you'll take advantage of the information that's available for free at (your website address). Thanks.

You can use these templates as written or as jumping-off points for creating your own letters. As an exclusive offer for readers of this book, if you would like me to personally critique your letters, just send an email to mark@gentlerainmarketing.com with the words "I'd like to take you up on your offer" in the subject line.

6.3 Email marketing

The wonderful thing about email is its versatility. Emails can be used to prospect for new affluent clients. They can also be used to stay in touch to and convert prospects into paying clients. In this chapter, we'll dig into how to use emails for these complimentary objectives, and I'll share some examples that you can adapt for your own marketing campaigns.

Let's start by discussing the use of emails to generate interest. There are a lot of email brokers that can provide you with lists of affluent prospects. These include ListGiant, LeadsPlease and Caldwell List Company. As with mailing lists, it's a good idea to shop around since there are often deals to be had.

Email lists are usually rented for a one-time mailing. That is, most often the provider sends out the email for you. They'll share a few names so you can check and make sure that the list is on target, but you are purchasing a one-time-only email blast. The only people you can send multiple emails to are those that respond to your offer and download your white paper, article or other lead magnet.

This all means that in order for cold-email marketing to work, you need to email a lot of people. By "a lot," I mean a very, very large group. Herein lies the problem with cold email marketing if you are targeting the affluent. The wealthy are not a mass market.

If you were selling fishing lures, email marketing might work really well. There are millions of fishermen. Likewise, you could probably sell a lot of golf gadgets through email. There are lots and lots of rabid golfers.

When it comes to wealthy individuals interested in art, worried about personal security, or curious about alternative investments, things are different. The numbers don't work in your favor, and this has all been a huge wind-up to tell you to not waste your time renting cold email lists. Does that mean cold mailing doesn't work for affluent marketing? Actually, it will work, but perhaps not in the way you think.

There is a very effective way to use email marketing, and it involves LinkedIn. I gave a detailed description of LinkedIn and its limitations earlier in the book, but let me shine a different light on the situation here. While it's true that you can't send mass emails through the platform, you can cold email a limited number of LinkedIn prospects and ask them to connect with you. At the time I'm writing this, the limit is 200 per week.

To use this to your advantage, identify a list of prospects on LinkedIn using any of the criteria they provide. This will only take a few minutes. Send an email through LinkedIn asking each of them to connect with you. Remember that the people you want to connect with get a lot of requests, so you need to communicate what's in it for them.

Don't use any of LinkedIn's suggested templates. They're done to death. Think about what each prospect is trying to accomplish and what they're interested in. The more specific you can be, the better. The goal is to have them say to themselves, "Ok, that makes sense. This might be someone who could be helpful." Here's what I send:

> Hi (first name),
>
> I know you get a lot of requests, but I believe that it would be beneficial for us to connect.
>
> We focus exclusively on building business relationships with the affluent. We've been doing this for thirty years, and some of our insights might be helpful to you.
>
> Mark

The second email is sent automatically after the person accepts the invitation to connect. This email is designed to move them out of the LinkedIn universe and on to your email list. Use your white paper, article, book or other content as the hook for doing this. Here's the email that I use, which is adaptable for most businesses:

> Hi (first name),
>
> I think that growing our businesses, building our brands, and getting a lot more new clients hinges in large part on the stories we tell.
>
> These are stories that communicate our expertise,

> stories about client success, and stories that make prospects say "I want to learn more." This is why I wanted to offer you a free copy of my Amazon #1 Best Seller *Unique Sales Stories*. It contains templates you can use immediately to build your brand and motivate prospective clients to take action. You can get your copy here: www.GentleRainMarketing.com.
>
> Talk soon,
> Mark

They go to the page on your website that promotes your offer, and they enter their name and email address to access it. Once they do that, they are a part of your community. It sounds simple, right? Unfortunately, not everyone will take you up on your offer the first time, so you'll often need to send a series of emails before they opt in to receive your lead magnet. For example, I send the following messages:

First follow-up:

> Hi (first name),
>
> Thanks for connecting with me. It's much appreciated.
>
> Obviously, I don't know what you're currently doing to brand your business, but I thought you might be interested in a free copy of my book *Unique Sales*

Stories: How to Get More Referrals & Differentiate Yourself From the Competition Through the Power of Stories.

It went to #1 on Amazon when it first came out, and I think you'll find it interesting and helpful. You can get it at www.gentlerainmarketing.com.

Thanks,
Mark

Second follow-up:

Hi (first name),

I was researching (name of their company), and I'm impressed with how you're positioning yourself in the marketplace.

One thing you might consider is sharing a select few stories about the firm, the key players, and perhaps some of your client successes. Because this can be so powerful, I thought you might be interested in a free copy of my book *Unique Sales Stories: How to Get More Referrals & Differentiate Yourself From the Competition Through the Power of Stories.*

It went to #1 on Amazon when it first came out, and I think you'll find it interesting and helpful. You can get it at https://bit.ly/3w6zqbA.

Thanks,
Mark

Third follow-up:

Hi (first name),

I don't know what vision you have for your business, but if one of your goals is to be recognized as a leading expert in your field, the following will be helpful.

A couple of years ago, I wrote a book specifically for business leaders who want to stop being the "best kept secret" in their industry and start being a highly sought-after expert. They want to be the person asked to speak at conferences and who gets interviewed by the leading business publications. You know what I'm talking about.

The book was a huge success. It went to #1 on Amazon and got great reviews. It explains how to use stories to build your brand and become that in-demand expert. A lot of business leaders (whose names you'd recognize) loved it and encouraged others to read it. It was all very flattering, but I'm writing to you today because **I'd like to offer you a free copy, which you can get HERE.**

The selfish reason for the offer is that I would like to start a business relationship with you, and I think

> that making this offer is a good way of accomplishing that. I hope that at some point (either now or in the future) you might be interested in talking with me about strategies for growing your business.
>
> I will leave it up to you to initiate that, but, in the meantime, I hope you will take me up on my offer for a free book. Many of your peers have found it valuable, and I think you will too. Again, **you can get your free copy HERE.**
>
> Thanks,
> Mark

I find that seventy-five to eighty percent of the people that receive these messages will eventually download the free book. That makes them part of my community and puts them on my email list, and I then use email to nurture the relationship, provide valuable information, and make offers.

When designing your own follow-up messages, you want to first determine your reason for sending the message. This sounds obvious, but it is so often overlooked. It might be that you want them to learn about a service you offer, or maybe you want them to get your book or read your blog. Don't begin writing until it's clear what the purpose is. What do you want the reader to do?

Also remember that emails can succeed or fail because of their subject lines. There are some great universal subject lines such as *This has always bothered me…*, *I have a quick question…*, and *Can you do me a favor?* that grab attention and create curiosity. For times when those aren't appropriate, the following are some of the top response-generating subjects that our clients have used over the years and some examples of their use:

How to…

- How to get more new clients
- How to be fascinating to others
- How to lose 14 lbs in the next 3 weeks
- How to get your baby to stop crying

5 (simple/unique/little-known) ways to (achieve something)

- *5 amazingly simple ways to reduce your costs by 45%*
- *5 little-known ways to end lower back pain*
- *5 unique remedies for social awkwardness*
- *5 little-known (but highly effective) things to do right now that will get you a lot more customers and clients*

The one (thing) to never (do something with)

- *The one exercise to never do*
- *The one email to never send*
- *The one food to never eat on a plane*

Avoid (this) to (that)

- *Avoid skipping breakfast to get a flatter stomach*
- *Avoid bad manners to attract women*
- *Avoid an unkempt lawn to sell your home in the next 14 days*

The biggest myth about (topic)

- *The biggest myth about collecting money that's owed you*
- *The biggest myth about being attractive to the opposite sex*
- *The biggest myth about being likable*
- *The biggest myth about retaining high-value employees*

After the subject line, the body of your email should have a conversational yet persuasive tone. In the body of the email, you want them to click on a link that takes them to a relevant page on your website. For this purpose, I encourage you to set up very specific pages on your site that each focus on one particular service that you offer. Following is the series of emails that I send. Feel free to adapt the messages to meet your specific needs.

First email:

Subject: Can I help?

Hi (first name),

Obviously, I don't know where you are in implementing your client-attraction system.

If the whole thing is set up and attracting consistent streams of great clients, congrats. I couldn't be happier for you. If you don't have your marketing system completely set up, though, and you'd like some help, we should talk.

Maybe you need some copywriting for emails, reports, or your website.

Maybe you need a great lead magnet, something that hooks the attention of prospective clients and starts the relationship.

Maybe you need a better, more up to date, website, one that's not just a brochure for your business but an online sales funnel that motivates visitors to "raise their hands" and express interest.

Maybe you need more, better-targeted traffic and more prospects entering the top of your conversion funnel.

Maybe you need a greater presence on social media including LinkedIn, Facebook, Instagram, and Twitter.

Maybe you need a more engaging follow-up sequence that moves prospects from being curious to hiring you.

Maybe you need a system that ensures that the only people you actually talk with are pre-qualified, are enthusiastically interested in what you offer, and can afford your services.

Maybe you need some technical help hooking everything up and making it work flawlessly .

Maybe you need a few of these things, and maybe you need it all. If you're a serious player with a reasonable budget for marketing, there's some additional information HERE. I look forward to helping you.

Talk soon,
Mark

Second email:

Subject: Implementation can be a pain

Hi (first name),

One of the biggest challenges preventing consultants, coaches and experts from achieving their business goals is the actual implementation of their plan.

If you're a bit stuck and would like some help, we should talk. We can pretty much do it all. We can design your website or sales funnel, perform copywriting for reports, emails, and landing pages, and set up and manage your social media presence. We can also do the technical stuff required to make it all work flawlessly. You tell me what you need and we'll get to work.

If you're a serious player with a reasonable budget for marketing, there's some additional information HERE.

Thanks,
Mark

Third email:

Subject: Are referrals really enough?

Hi (first name),

When I ask consultants, experts and coaches how they're getting new clients, I invariably hear about word of mouth and referrals.

Quite frankly, that might be fine for you. It all depends upon what goals you have for your business. However, the truth of the matter is that if you have aspirations to really be a player in your field, your existing base of contacts most likely won't get you there, and neither will all of your "friends" or your "network" on Facebook or LinkedIn. You need a client-attraction system.

I'm probably not telling you anything you don't already know, but implementing such a system can be a challenge. There's design, copywriting, and all the technical stuff. It's easy to understand why so many consultants, experts and coaches never actually get their client-attraction system implemented, and this is why I wanted to reach out to you.

My team and I can do everything for you. It could be anything from writing some simple sales copy all the way up to completely designing and implementing your entire system and implementing a highly targeted advertising program. You just let us know how we can be helpful.

If you're a serious player with a reasonable budget for marketing, there's some additional information HERE.

Thanks,
Mark

To sum it all up, email, when selectively used, can be a viable tool for prospecting. However, its real value is as a communication tool for addressing the "know, like and trust factors" that are critically important for converting prospects into paying clients.

6.4 Cold and warm telephone prospecting

I'll admit that I have very mixed feelings about cold calling. The affluent are heavily protected from unsolicited phone calls so, at least in theory, it shouldn't work. But alas, it does work, as long as you follow some guidelines.

Ideally, you don't want to make an entirely cold call to a prospect. Although we will discover shortly that this can work, common sense dictates that your results will be a lot better if you're calling a warm prospect rather than someone with whom you have had absolutely no previous contact. CEO Clark Todderly's real estate investment team uses the phone as their primary means of selling to affluent investors. He says:

> To say that we cold call would be a bit misleading. Everyone we call has requested some information about us, whether it be a sales brochure or, more likely, one of our newsletters or articles. So, I guess you would say that we're calling a warm prospect.
>
> We have a very robust lead-generation process whereby we promote our quarterly *State of the Commercial Real Estate Investment Market* both online and off. We run ads in trade publications and enthusiast magazines that we know our affluent prospects read as well as banner ads on high-traffic blogs. The follow-up messages we send after someone requests the information are primarily focused on getting a viable phone number. We've found over the years that asking for a number at the beginning usually results in just

> getting a bogus one or an outright refusal. However, if we can build trust with our ongoing communication, that reluctance eventually goes away.
>
> Since our follow-up is done exclusively on the phone, we have an entire marketing system designed to get that one piece of information. The added benefit of this is that when we get a valid phone number, we know that we have someone who is really interested in what we offer.

He underscores an important point: you must think of affluent sales and marketing as a series of steps. Following up on the phone with a prospect who has requested information or who has downloaded a lead magnet is quite different from calling someone completely out of the blue.

Regardless of whether it is a warm or completely cold call, the first five seconds are crucial. Your success or failure depends on what occurs during that time. In many ways, the first five seconds of a call are like the first sentence of your sales letter. You're either going to get the other person interested or lose their interest entirely. This is true whether you're calling housewives or millionaires.

Success with cold calling depends on both your inner confidence and what you actually say. Although both are important, success in cold calling depends more on the first than the second. Unfortunately, as legendary marketer John Carlton says, "Most people sell from their heels. They seek not to offend rather than to persuade." You must convey authority from the moment you pick up the phone. This is why becoming one of the elite experts in your field (and knowing deep down that you are one) is crucially important. This gives you the confidence that you'll need when you deliver your message.

The more you develop white papers, write books, blog, and build your community of followers, the more confidence you'll have when picking up the phone. Don't for a moment believe that you have to have a certain number of years' experience before you can brand yourself as an expert. It has nothing to do with chronological age. Becoming a recognized expert has everything to do with the effort you make to position yourself and build your brand.

Golfers have what they call "swing thoughts," which are things that they keep top of mind when they go out to play a round. An example might be "Keep my head down throughout the entire swing" or "Make sure I keep the club head moving after contact with the ball." You need something like a swing thought, too.

Your swing thought is like battle armor. It's what you put on mentally before you pick up the phone. Maybe you remind yourself that you are the best person to help the people you're calling achieve their goals. You're the one who can best help them get what they most want in life. Remind yourself that you are a person worth listening to. That's an important self-belief for any marketing effort, but it's crucial when cold calling.

An often-overlooked element of success in cold calling is body language. You might think that it's not important since your prospect can't see you, but you would be wrong. Lester Minnings manages a call center that focuses on alternative assets. His prospective clients are both wealthy and financially savvy. He says:

> We sell a sophisticated financial option to very smart and knowledgeable investors. We are light years away from the stereotypical boiler room that you see in movies. Despite that, what we do is hard work. There's no getting around it.
>
> We work off a script, but what has made the biggest difference is focusing on body language and personal attire. It may sound unusual since our sales team rarely meets with clients face to face, but we insist that they dress professionally. If you put on a sharp business outfit, you'll feel more confident than if you're making calls dressed in jeans and a tee shirt.
>
> Body language is also critically important. That's why our walls are covered in floor-to-ceiling mirrors. The reflection gives energy to the room, and it enables our team members to see themselves when they're making calls. It's not vanity. It's not "Boy do I look great." What it does is reinforce the importance of sitting or standing up straight, using hand gestures, and making sure that your body is aligned with the words that are coming out of your mouth.

Jonathan St. Edwards manages a team of thirty-five financial advisors. The minimum requirement for their clients is to have

$1 million in assets under management. What makes this team interesting is that 85% of their new business comes from cold calling. Jonathan explains:

> I know that the common wisdom is that cold calling doesn't work, especially with the wealthy. I've been doing this for thirty years, and despite what people say and all the new technology, cold calling is still our go-to strategy.
>
> One thing that works for us is that we do our calls in a bullpen so everyone can hear each other. Maintaining a high energy level is crucial since you are going to hear no after no after no. Trying to cold call by yourself? I don't know how anyone could possibly do that.
>
> We work off of scripts and spend a lot of time training on how to deliver the presentation. Although the scripts are pretty detailed, I encourage everyone to adapt them to their individual voice.
>
> The real key with a cold calling strategy, especially when you're focused as we are on the affluent, is persistence. We will simply not give up. Sometimes it takes twenty, thirty…I think we even had one instance where a lady on our team called a prospect fifty-seven times before she finally connected. What we eventually hear most often is that "Hey, you called me dozens of times. I figured I'd see what you guys

> were all about."
>
> We hedge our bets by also making a lot of our calls early in the morning and late in the day. Early in the morning is the best. We find that if you make the call before their assistant gets in, the person we want to talk with often picks up the phone themselves.
>
> We also integrate our direct mail program with the cold calling. If it's someone we really want to do business with, we'll send fruit baskets or some sort of cheesy gift with a card that says "Twenty-two calls and counting. I really think you'd like to hear what we have to say." That's really effective.

What's frustrating about cold calling is the amount of sheer repetition required. Designer Tom Ford famously called New York fashion boss Cathy Hardwick every day for a full month asking for the chance to work with her. Finally, she agreed to an interview and subsequently hired him. Thus, the good news is that cold calling will work for gaining access to the affluent. The question is whether you are committed enough to make the number of calls that might be necessary. Music manager Scooter Braun makes the following analogy:

> Imagine that a baseball team runs a promotion during a game. Anyone who can get a hit off of their Cy Young winning pitcher will get $100,000. Now, most of the people in the stands won't even line up

> for a try. That's the way it is in real life. Most people sit on the sidelines.
>
> But a line does form. The first couple of people go up to the plate, take a couple of swings, and then pass the bat to the next person in line. That goes on for a while. Again, in real life, most people that try to do something don't really commit. They'll take a stab at being successful but fold pretty quickly.
>
> Finally, one guy comes up and takes his turn. Five swings. Ten swings. Fifty swings. The crowd is booing. They're yelling, "Sit down! Give someone else a chance!" But he stands in and continues to swing. Despite the noise, despite the discouragement, he keeps going until he finally hits the ball…and the crowd goes crazy. He gets a standing ovation. All the haters are now fans.
>
> People are quick to tell you that you're crazy to try something, and it's hard to tune out the negatives. It's really difficult to stay motivated when you don't have any sign that if you stick with it you will be successful. You just have to have faith. That's what it takes if you truly want to be successful.

That's a very valuable lesson for anyone who wants to develop relationships with the affluent. It's of particular relevance when cold calling.

Regarding the role of scripts, almost everyone who successfully builds relationships with the affluent through cold calling uses scripts to some extent. The script should answer the prospect's natural question "What's in it for me?" It should give them an idea of what you can offer them and how your product or service can help them.

With those goals in mind, let's get to work and create your first script. The first part of any cold calling script is the introduction. You tell the person on the other end of the line what your name is and where you work. The key is to speak naturally, conversationally, and with restrained enthusiasm. You don't want to come across as hyper, but rather as someone making a friendly greeting at a social event.

The next part of your script is about the connection. You give some kind of justification for making the call by explaining your association with them. You might say something like "You may remember that we met last Friday at the Friends of Weymouth Dinner" or "If you recall, you downloaded our article *How To Raise Well-Adjusted Kids When You're Extremely Wealthy*."

Once you've calmly introduced yourself and given your pretext for calling, you mention outcomes. You say something like "We specialize in helping (people like them) (attain outcome one), (attain outcome two), and (attain outcome three)." You will have to use your judgment to decide how many outcomes to mention. Typically, giving any number of outcomes from one to three is fine, and then you'll immediately move on to qualifying.

To qualify the prospect, you'll say something like "If you have just a minute, I'd like to ask you a couple of quick questions so I don't waste your time." Your questions at this point should focus on the needs of the prospect and what, if anything, they are currently doing to solve their problems. You might ask:

- Is it fair to say this is (something they want to achieve or want to avoid)?
- What are you doing currently to (address this issue)?
- How are your current efforts working out?
- When are you looking to (take action or implement a solution)?
- On a scale from one to ten, how important is (this thing) to you?

Not all of these questions will be relevant to every person you call. Based on what you sell, you should modify the questions or add to the list as appropriate. Try to limit the number of questions you ask an individual to three or four, however, so that it doesn't come across like an interrogation.

Follow the qualifying questions with a transition. In this section, you shift the focus from their problems to your solutions. When doing this, it's very important to focus on the benefits that other people are getting from your solutions. Mentioning the results that others have achieved or how the solution is used by someone famous are always beneficial.

Once you've presented your solutions and their benefits, you want to check their understanding by asking something like "Does this all make sense?" or "Are you with me so far?" This is important for a few reasons. The first is the psychological benefit that comes whenever another person says "Yes" to what you are proposing. Another is that you want to make sure that your messaging is on track and that your solutions align with their goals. Yet another is that asking positive, closed-ended questions keeps people verbally engaged, which reduces the likelihood of the call sounding like a canned sales pitch.

Finally, having confirmed that they understand that you have an effective solution to their problem, you move on to the close. The most effective close is simple. You just reiterate the problem, communicate what you can do for them, and tell them what you want them to do. This is the same formula used in great direct-response sales letters, which are often referred to as "cold calling in print." In that case, it's described as "Here's what I've got, here's what it will do for you, and here's what I want you to do next."

The reality is that the first time you attempt to close them, they will probably want to ask additional questions. That's fine. This phase is sometimes called "the loop." You'll answer the question but continually bring the focus to the benefits without getting mired down in the features or details of your solution. You should be prepared to work your way through three loops before the typical prospect says they are ready to take the next step.

Having now assembled your script, you need to practice before you actually pick up the phone. Note that when I say practice, I mean that you need to practice out loud. There is an enormous difference between running a presentation in your head and physically speaking the words. In your mind, you're always clear, concise and articulate, but when you first say something, it can often come across as hesitant and dull. You need to develop a "mouth feel" for your pitch, so don't overlook this step.

An interesting twist on cold calling has been used by Steven McDougall, who runs a security company that caters to very affluent families. As he describes it:

> We used cold calling extensively for many years with I guess what could be called a traditional approach. Back a few years ago, we shifted our marketing focus to publishing articles and white papers on how to secure art collections and other valuables. This gave us an idea.
>
> Instead of calling and asking about their current security system, my team started calling with the focus on interviewing people for an article about estate security, the issues they faced, what solutions were working, what was not…that sort of thing. The percentage of people who were willing to speak with us tripled from what we were doing previously.
>
> The great thing about this approach was that it made for a very easy transition to finding out about their current security system and any issues they were facing. We offer a free assessment and are able to drop a few names about the types of clients we work with, so this approach was very effective at advancing the

sales process to the next step.

Assuming I've convinced you how valuable it can be to write books, you could use that process as a basis for applying this twist yourself. For example, the following script demonstrates how you might open a cold call by using book research as a hook.

> Hi (first name), this is (your name and company). Recently, I've been working on a book about (a subject), and it occurred to me that it would be great to get your perspective on the topic. If you have a minute for a few questions, I think your responses would be very helpful to my readers.

You'll then ask them five or six questions along the lines of:

- What are you currently doing?
- How satisfied are you with that?
- If you could change one thing about your current system, what would that be?

When writing this type of cold-call script, you'll base the transition on the questions that you ask. You should be able to uncover numerous wants and needs that you can meet.

Now that we've discussed what to do and ways to do it, I'll just mention a few general points to keep in mind. First, you want to introduce yourself with energy and confidence, and you have to make sure to articulate your name and your company. We've all received calls from "Bnrblbll from Nmnnusr," and you know that this kills the call from the get go.

Second, realize that trying to create rapport with the first couple of sentences makes the call sound forced. That said, be alert and pick up clues so that you can deviate from the script and personalize the conversation. For example, you might say things like:

- I see you graduated from XYZ University. How did you like it?
- Congrats on being at ABC company for X years. How did you get started there?
- Kudos on your recent promotion. How's the new role going?

Third, don't say "I," but rather "we" or "you." Psychologists have long known that the use of "we" gets prospects to engage with you more quickly. It emphasizes the collaborative nature of the solution you are proposing. The focus of the call is on the benefits they get from you, not how great you are. You focus on them by saying things like:

- Are you experiencing issues with…
- What roadblocks are you encountering with…
- Would it benefit you if…

Fourth, you always want to be respectful of their time. After asking one or two questions, transition to "I'd love to ask you some additional questions, but I want to be respectful of your time. Is now good, or is there a better time for us to continue our conversation?"

The fifth point is obvious: you will have to anticipate rejections. You even know already what the most common objections will be. The first is obviously money. You will also hear quite often that a prospect is already working with one of your competitors. In a given field, there are usually three or four objections that come up repeatedly, but they are not a secret, and you can prepare for them.

If they mention that they are working with a competitor, take the opportunity to probe and find out what's working and what's not. You might ask "If there was one thing that you wish they would do differently or better, what would that be?" When money inevitably comes up, the typical issue is that no one wants to be the first to name a price. In this situation, I'd recommend a great technique that Mahan Kalsa covers in his excellent book *Let's Get Real or Let's Not Play*. You say to the prospect:

> We've been talking a lot about what you're trying to accomplish, and if I'm hearing your correctly, the main issues for you are (three to four things that you've identified as the key challenges they are facing).
>
> Obviously, the question that you're asking yourself is "How much will this cost me?" The answer is

> that I don't really know. However, I can tell you that clients similar to you who are trying to (accomplish similar goals) typically invest between X and Y. Can you see yourself falling somewhere in that range?

Like any other skill, telephone skill requires practice to perfect. While some people are naturally more effective over the phone than others, there is no reason why anyone can't use the telephone as an important part of their overall sales process. The real key, which applies to almost everything I've shared with you, is that you need to take what you've learned here and adapt it to fit your personal style. Communicating your value by being your enhanced, authentic self is the real secret to success.

Chapter 7:
Turning prospects into clients

This is a short chapter since, if you've done everything in the preceding chapters, closing the sale will be relatively quick. Awareness is good. Building your brand is good. Everything I've been sharing with you up to this point is good. It all means nothing, though, if we don't convert prospects into paying clients. So, let's discuss how to do that.

First, let's do a quick review of where we've been so far on this journey.

- You've identified the specific affluent niche market you want to focus on, and you've developed an in-depth profile of your ideal client.
- You've developed a list of wealthy prospects using a combination of push marketing and pull marketing strategies.
- You've built credibility and enormous good will by sending your prospects relevant and inter-

esting information that develops the know, like and trust factors that are crucial for building relationships.

- You've repeatedly and consistently made the offer for a free consultation, and you've provided compelling reasons for them to take you up on that offer.
- You've set up the form with which they can request a consultation, and the form contains questions to ensure that you only spend time talking to your ideal prospects.

All of that takes us to the last step. How do you convert these prospects into clients? Based on the information they provide in the form, you should have a very good idea about how you will advise them during the call. Since they've requested the meeting, you know they're interested. It's in this conversation that you'll turn them from a prospect into a client. You're going to use a process known in sales circles as the "collaborative close." This extremely non-salesy sales close is all about being helpful and asking questions. I know it will all sound too simple to be true, but I'm going to share with you now a scripted blueprint for the call.

To begin, we ask some questions to find out where they are now, where they want to be, and what result they hope to achieve by working with you. You can ask, "If we were having this conversation twelve months from today and you were looking back, what would need to have happened for you to be happy with your results?" I learned to ask this question from a book called *The Dan Sullivan Question*. It's a great approach, and I highly recommend the book to you. This question makes the prospect think twelve months into the future, picture himself having worked with you as a client, and tell you exactly what needs to happen for him to be happy. That gives you a very clear idea of where he wants to be.

Next, to find out where he is now and what he wants to achieve, you can ask, "Do you think that would be helpful?" or "Do you think that might work?" With these questions, you figure out the steps he needs to take in order to get to where he wants to go. You're not telling him what he should do. You're merely suggesting ideas. Once you've asked all of your questions and gotten all of his answers, simply reiterate the steps you've already discussed and position that as a plan of action. Having done that, ask your super-hard-sell closing question.

The collaborative close is adaptable for any business, but the following hypothetical conversation with a financial advisor will give you a sense for how it all sounds.

> Me: If we were having this conversation twelve months from today and you were looking back, what would need to have happened for you to be happy with your results?
>
> Prospect: Well, I'd want to have $20 million in assets under management.

Me: Okay. How much do you have under management now?

Prospect: I have about $5 million.

Now that you know where they are and where they want to go, it's time to start building the path to get there.

Me: I understand. What's the average amount of assets of your current clients?

Prospect: There's a range, but overall my clients average around $500,000.

Me: Okay, so we can either focus on getting you more clients who are similar to the ones you have now, or we can focus on getting clients with more assets. Which would you like to focus on?

Prospect: I'd really like clients with $2 million to invest.

Me: Fine. So that means that we need to develop a plan to get you an additional ten clients. Does that sound right?

Now that you know what their goals are, you can collaboratively build a plan together. The next step is to create the blueprint. You've identified the prospect's goals, so you'll start suggesting activities that will help achieve the wanted results.

Me: You know, based on what you've told me, it sounds like we should implement a referral program with your wealthiest clients.

Prospect: Yeah, I think that's a good idea.

Me: It occurs to me that it also sounds like we could upgrade the quality of your clients by getting you featured in the business press.

Prospect: Yeah, that's exactly what we've just discussed earlier. I think I mentioned that.

Me: Then going forward, you could offer on your website that article you wrote as a lead magnet to build your community of prospective clients.

Prospect: Yeah, that sounds good.

Me: What do you think about hosting an intimate client dinner with some joint venture partners such as an estate attorney and a CPA? You could choose a topic that's an interest of one of your affluent clients. Do you think art investing or wine collecting would work?

Prospect: I've thought about that in the past but never pulled the trigger. Yes, I think that could definitely work.

Me: Okay, let's put that on our list of potential strategies.

Remember, you're not pushing any agenda on them. You're just asking questions like "What do you think would happen if we did this? What are your ideas around this? Do you think this idea might work?" Since you're an expert in your field, you know a lot of things that a client would really benefit from. That's what you walk your prospect through, always asking "What do you think would happen if we…"

The next step is the pre-close. Once you have identified the strategies that will get the prospect the results they want, you'll summarize them as a prescription.

Me: I want to make sure that I've got everything that we talked about. We've discussed:

- Starting a referral program
- Putting articles in the business press
- Adding a lead magnet to your website
- Hosting an intimate client dinner with JV partners

> Is there anything else that comes to mind that might help us achieve your goal of ten new clients?

Once you've come up with an agreed-upon, comprehensive list of what needs to be done, you'll ask your pre-closing question.

> Me: Does that sound like an effective plan of action to you? Do you think we could get you an additional ten clients if we implemented this plan?

Basically, you've just given them all the answers they gave you, you created a plan of action out of them, and you asked a pre-closing question that links back to the goal they told you they wanted to achieve. Again, note that you're not pushing any solution. You're just asking questions.

After the pre-close question, we proceed with the close. Assuming the prospect has answered in the affirmative, I would recommend the following bad-ass close:

> Me: Would you like me to help you implement this plan going forward?

I get an affirmative answer to this question 80% of the time, and I'm not the only one. That 80% number is consistent among my clients who have implemented this approach in over two dozen different niche industries. Keep in mind that this close only works because of what preceded it. All the steps that we've discussed need to be in place in order for this to work.

You don't have to be a salesperson, and it's fine if you're not. Nobody wants to be sold to anyhow. Rather, they want to be helped. The bottom line is that if you can approach this conversation with the goal of helping your prospects achieve their goals, you can attract as many affluent clients as you desire. All you need is a structured way of communicating how you can help, and you now have that.

Chapter 8:
Final thoughts

I thought I'd wrap up this book by mentioning a couple of challenges that you are likely to hear. One tribal characteristic of the wealthy is that they are very straightforward and quick to get to the point. They'll ask you the tough questions that others may shy away from, so you need to be prepared.

The first question to expect is "Why should I work with you instead of with one of your competitors, and why is working with you better than doing nothing?" The follow-up challenge is "Can you sell me on what you, and you alone, add to the solution?" I'm always surprised that so few people spend time thinking about how to respond to questions like this. I suppose it's because they're difficult, and everyone just hopes that they won't get put on the spot.

Unfortunately, except in one scenario that I'll cover shortly, the affluent *will* corner you, and you will need to respond. Answering such questions requires having a detailed understanding of your competition, what their strengths are, and how you are different. You don't necessarily need to say that you're better. That's a judgment that only the person you are speaking with can make. However, you need to be able to articulate why you are different and, by inference, perhaps a better alternative.

You'll score points if you can respond to the tough questions with a variation of "If I had to guess, since you're talking with me, you're also probably talking with..." That sets you up to be able to discuss the differences between your approach and those of your competitors. It also establishes you as a knowledgeable expert in your field. It's sort of a variation on the conversational name dropping that's done in social situations to ascertain whether you're a member of the tribe.

The trick is balance. You don't want to come across as arrogant with a lot of bluster, yet you don't want to hide your light under the proverbial bushel basket. As in any sales-orientated conversation, you need to have an understanding of the desired outcomes. What do they want? What do they fear? Those are the twin levers that should guide your responses.

You want to make sure that you aren't just parroting something that they've heard a million times before. On the surface, a financial advisor knows that his clients want to increase their wealth and that they fear losing their money. This is true, but it's also really obvious. You need to dig deeper and come up with more nuanced things to say that will differentiate you from the others they may be talking with.

At some point, you have to move beyond showing that you understand the fears and desires of your prospective affluent client. You eventually need to communicate the reason that you are the right choice. Bad reasons include things like "willingness to work hard," "going the extra mile," or any of those trite replies.

There really aren't cookie cutter answers to questions about what makes you so special. It will require some critical thinking on your part to figure out how to truly communicate that you are the best choice. If you can't come up with good reasons, that's a major piece of data. As the saying goes in poker, if you can't figure out who the sucker is, then it's you. If you can't come up with answers that you can communicate with conviction, your odds of successfully attracting affluent clients are severely compromised.

The good news is that by taking the time to really think about these questions and formulate answers, you will separate yourself from the 95% who never do so. The sad truth is that people are fundamentally lazy, and they like solutions that require very little thinking. You are more than capable of coming up with great responses. You just need to devote the time and do the mental heavy lifting that is required. Don't despair if you find that you really struggle with this. Most people do. To give you a hand, there is a free offer at the end of this chapter that is guaranteed to help.

Going back to the two major questions that you need to be prepared for, don't forget the prospect's option to do nothing. You need to be able to communicate the consequences that are likely to occur if that path is taken. I like to string together consequences and say "If you do nothing, then (this) is likely to happen. If that happens, then (this other thing) is likely to happen, and if that happens…"

You can see how this plays out. In one of my workshops, we used to have participants take strings of consequences to their logical ends as an exercise. Usually within five iterations of "if this happens then this other thing is likely to happen," either the company goes out of business or the person dies. The exercise is a lot of fun in a macabre sort of way, but it teaches a valuable lesson nonetheless.

Now, I mentioned earlier that you can avoid having the "why you" questions come up at all. Such circumstances are created by your marketing. Dan Kennedy once said that "Nobody pays a lot of money to talk to the guru at the bottom of the hill." That's a point worth thinking about. A lot of people, especially when they are marketing their services to the very rich, come across as needy. I know you think that you don't, but the reality is that most do. That's why you get these tough questions in the first place. You haven't done a particularly good job of positioning yourself in the marketplace.

This is tough, but you really need to work on it. In order to successfully do business with the very rich, you need to have an attitude of being their peer. The reality is that you're not their peer in terms of wealth, but you have another card to play: your expertise. There is a fine line between self-confidence and arrogance, and you don't want to cross that line, but you need to position yourself and your business in a way that communicates that you are damn good at what you do.

You must also truly believe that. I'll give you an analogy that, while it isn't perfect, should make my point. The American

Express Centurion Card (also known as the Black Card) is the Rolls Royce of credit cards. Hardly anyone has one, and it has developed mythical status. Supposedly, Mark Cuban set the Guinness World Record for the largest ever credit card charge when he used his Black Card to purchase a private jet.

The point is, most credit card companies try far too hard to do business with you. How many pitches from Capital One have you seen or received? Even if you're a huge Samuel L. Jackson fan, you have to admit that they're annoying with their never-ending commercials and pop-up ads. By contrast, the Black Card is obtained by invitation only. It's like being tapped by the most prestigious and secretive fraternity or society on campus.

Amex won't reveal what the invitation criteria are. They'll only confirm that it costs $5,000 to get the card and $2500 annually to keep it. Look at how it's positioned. It's rarely seen but always recognized. It's available by invitation only. It confers a level of service that can be extended only to select individuals worldwide.

Think about all of this for a moment from a marketing perspective. The card is elite. It's aspirational…but it's just a freaking credit card. It has no special powers. You just get to charge stuff with it. It's all positioning and marketing, and that's what I want you to think about when presenting yourself.

Given everything that you've learned from this book, your next step is to develop your strategy, your blueprint for how you are going to position yourself in the market. What does this entail? You might:

- Develop a detailed profile of your ideal candidate so that he or she sees a reflection of themselves in your marketing materials.
- Complete the exercise on developing your network and, using some of the templates I gave you, reach out to establish or reestablish a relationship.
- Host an intimate client event, perhaps with some joint venture partners, addressing a topic that you know your prospective wealthy clients are interested in.
- Write some articles, a white paper, or even a book that will position you as one of the experts in your field.
- Get the word out about your expertise with a weekly blog, posts on social media, YouTube videos and shares to LinkedIn groups.
- Set up your website so that it invites prospects to connect with you by offering them something of value.
- Utilize targeted direct mail and email to attract new prospective affluent clients.
- Make a compelling description of the value individuals will receive by taking you up on your offer of a free consultation, and in that conversation, develop a joint blueprint for success by following the script I provided you.

If you do all of those things–heck, if you did just some of those things–do you think you would have as many affluent clients as you want? Of course you would. So, let me leave you with one final question. Would you like some assistance in implementing that plan? If so, go to GentleRainMarketing.com, and let's see if maybe I can help you. Regardless of whether you take me up on that offer, I sincerely want to thank you for taking the time to read this book. I appreciate you, and I wish you much continued success.

Mark Satterfield
mark@gentlerainmarketing.com

P.S. If you did find this book to be helpful, a quick review on Amazon would be greatly appreciated. Thanks!

Made in United States
Troutdale, OR
10/29/2024

24270922R00122